Your Creative Power of Love

World Change Begins with You

Tommy Knestrick

Your Creative Power of Love
World Change Begins with You
(Revision of the book *Be Spiritual, Love Age Needs You*)

Copyright © 2012 by Tommy Knestrick

Writing and drawings by Tommy Knestrick
Edited by Loretta Medenciy
Cover by Rob Knestrick
Graphic art by Andrew Knestrick

All rights reserved. Portions of this book may be freely quoted or reprinted up to 500 words without permission, providing credit is given to Tommy Knestrick, *Your Creative Power of Love*, Copyright © 2012. Otherwise, no other part of this book may be reproduced, stored in a retrieval system, or transmitted in any form by any means mechanical, electronic, photographic, or recording for public or private use.

The author of this book does not dispense medical advice or prescribe the use of any technique as a form of treatment for physical, emotional, or medical problems without the advice of a physician. The author's intent is only to provide general information to help you in your quest for social and spiritual well-being. If you use the information in this book, which is your right, the author and the publisher assume no responsibility for your actions.

ISBN 13: 978-0615624624 10: 0615624626

Love Age Press
P. O. Box 292987
Sacramento, California 95829
Printed in the United States of America

DEDICATION

To my wife and spiritual partner, Audrey, who is partly responsible for helping me learn to live a life creating the power of love.

To my four children, Rob, BJ, Scott, and Kim and my four grandchildren Darrell, Jenn, Andrew, and Sean. I am so thankful the Divine helped place them in my life to give the lessons and help needed to be more loving.

To those with the courage and commitment to live with love in their everyday lives during a difficult period of history, for living with higher spiritual vibrations of love in their relationships, for changing themselves and the world, and for advancing the Love Age.

Contents

In Gratitude viii
Introduction 1

SHIFT I   EGO SELF TO A DIVINE SELF

1. *Paradigm Shift to a Divine Self* 13
2. *Recognizing the Ego* 25
3. *Ego is Fear-based* 39
4. *Love flows from the Divine Within* 53

SHIFT II   EGO POLARIZATION TO SPIRITUAL ONENESS

5. *You're an Energy Being United with Others* 67
6. *Energy Fields and Spiritual Oneness* 81

SHIFT III   GOOD-FOR-ME TO GOOD-FOR-ALL

7. *Amanda Dream—Love's Turning Point* 93
8. *Is Win/Win the Same as Good-for-All?* 111
9. *Is Love All You Need?* 121

SHIFT IV   EGO-CREATING TO LOVEAGE-CREATING

10. *Ego-creating Phases* 135
11. *Transitional Phase* 163
12. *LoveAge-creating Phases* 181

SHIFT V   EGO AGE TO LOVE AGE

13. *Is the World Ending or Shifting?* 195
14. *Evolution of Awareness* 215
15. *Importance of Being a LoveAge-creator* 227
    Appendix—Love Age Commitment Forms 247
    Contact Information 253
    Index 255

In Gratitude

One of the attributes of living with love is to be grateful. When I thought about how this book became reality, I realized I had a lot to be grateful for.

Foremost, I'm thankful for my wife, Audrey, who served as my spiritual partner along our life's journey, which had many difficult and happy times. She was a bright star of compassion that helped direct my heart toward the light of the Divine. Most of the time, she was aware that our old dogmatic religious paths had lost their usefulness, and she helped pull me along to higher levels. As a spiritual partner, she provided ample lessons that sparked my ego responses, which I had to learn to recognize and replace. She also served as an example of the love needed to help me mature spiritually. She was a significant part of the story that helped me co-create or be a spiritual being of love. My wish for you is that you have a spiritual partner to help you become more loving, as I did.

I'm grateful for our four children—Rob, BJ, Scott, and Kim—who selected us, through divine guidance, to be members of our family's lessons and experiences. They helped me, during my spiritual struggles, not only to learn needed lessons but to provide some of them too. We are a close-knit family, and they were not only subject matter for the book, but they also helped edit it. I want to give a special thanks to Rob, who created the structure for the book's front and back cover. Our last name, Knestrick is pronounced with a silent "K" (*"nes·trick"*).

Usually on Sundays, my children and grandchildren (Jenn, Andrew, and Sean) meet to read drafts of chapters, and they would provide needed editorial feedback. I was surprised at times when my grandchildren provided valuable inputs to improve the book. I want to give special thanks to

Andrew who as a high school student created the graphic arts for this book.

I am grateful for the Methodist Church, Quakers, Edgar Cayce, Eckankar™, and others that were there when I needed them for my spiritual unfoldment. They all had a place in my spiritual development that helped make this book possible, even though I am no longer associated with any of them now.

I am also grateful for the Marianna, Pennsylvania discussion group that read copies of my draft chapters. My sister, Ruth Ann and her husband Paul were members of the group along with my cousin, Betty. Paul's mother, Loretta, and her two daughters, Bev and Monica. I had been asking the Divine for someone who could edit my book other than my immediate family. From the Marianna book discussion group, Loretta, a retired English teacher, was provided. I am deeply thankful for all the editing she has done to make this book more readable and grammatically correct.

I am grateful to Don A. Singletary, who helped with information on self-publishing to get this book ready for publication. I am also thankful for CreateSpace, a POD publisher. They are truly a blessing for those who want to self-publish.

Most importantly, I am grateful for receiving the Divine's help. When I started to write this book about creating with the power of love, I did not allow the Divine to be my writing partner. Gradually, I was given lessons along the way about being a co-creative writer and about the need to partner with the Divine. These lessons opened up an inner connection with the Divine, where I eventually received its inner wisdom. I hope these experiences made the book more helpful for initiating love in your life.

The term ECKANKAR is a trademark of ECKANKAR P.O. Box 27300, Minneapolis, MN 55427

Introduction

I saw the documentary film, *I Am*, that was created and directed by Tom Shadyac, but do not confuse it with the movie, *I Am, of* the same name. Tom was the Hollywood director of *Liar Liar, The Nutty Professor, Bruce Almighty*, and other movies. After he had a life threatening accident, he started questioning his Hollywood style of living and gave it up in order to live in a trailer park, where he also started to seek answers to important questions about life.

In the film, *I Am*, he interviewed scientists, thinkers, and people who were interested in implementing paradigm shifts to change the world from conflict to cooperation. He asked two questions, and the first one was, *What is wrong with our world?* Shadyac's final answer for this question was, "I AM."

This was the same answer I had for this question, except I was a little more specific about the "I AM." It was my ego self with its habits of conflict, fear, unconscious reactions, unhappiness, intolerance, attachments, and doing what's good-for-me that underlie the problems of my personal life as well as the world's consciousness and problems.

Tom Shadyac's second question was, *What can we do about it?* Again his basic answer was, "I AM." We are responsible to make personal life changes usually in small steps that will eventually help change our self and the world. For Shadyac, he believed he was responsible for what was wrong with the world and was also the one responsible for changing it.

I, too, addressed the question of what I could do about the world to make it a better place as well as to stop the trend toward world conflict, unhappiness, and the world's possible destruction. My answer was *to change myself first by using the creative power of love, which would in turn help change the world*. By being peaceful, cooperative, loving, joyful, and free, and by consciously choosing intentions and using good-for-all motivations, I would not only change my personal life for the better, but I would also affect the rest of the world. By changing myself, I too helped change the world. It's that simple.

This book discusses five major shifts in consciousness that I experienced in transitioning to a more loving self while affecting the world for the greater good. To start with, I had to make a shift from identifying myself as the ego self to realizing myself as the Divine Self. This became one of my life's purposes. Secondly, I had to change the way the ego self separated itself from others, from nature, and from the Divine, to attain a consciousness where I would live in a state of oneness with all. Also, I shifted the ego consciousness of desiring and doing what is good-for-me to a consciousness where the good-for-All motivation thrived. The fourth shift was a personal transformation from ego-creating to LoveAge-creating.

Finally, the personal and collective changes from all of the above shifts combined to move me out of the Ego Age consciousness to the Love Age consciousness. These, plus a

Introduction

few other shifts that will be discussed in another book, are what helped me live and create life with love.

All of these shifts in consciousness had to happen first of all within me. This is why it is so important for you to live from the spiritual love that flows from within. If you change your ego consciousness, you also change the world's ego institutions. This change happens by means of interconnected energy webs of love pulsating from your creative chain reactions of love to broader physical, social, and ecological webs. Quantum scientists are aware of how all matter and its energies interconnect throughout multiple layers of interacting systems. This is why shifting into the Love Age requires changing yourself first, rather than trying to change others. So what's right with the world? It is *me and you living and creating with love*. Be a divine being of love filled with divine wisdom, power, and peace in order to automatically help change yourself as well as the rest of the world for the greater good.

Are you creating with the power of love???

I have used questions throughout the book to make you pause and think about whether the action or principle discussed applies to an experience you had in your life. I have also used three question marks to emphasize the importance of some of the question.

When I originally thought about writing this book, I just wanted to share experiences with my religious group about how I learned to co-create with love. After reading other authors and observing what was going on in the world, I realized that my own experiences were part of a larger shift in consciousness. I then decided to integrate my personal experiences into what others saw as an evolutionary leap into what I call the age of love. However, this shift is not a sure thing since it depends on enough people consciously choosing to change their own consciousness. If you make this commitment, you can be a pioneer of the Love Age and help usher it in.

Would you like to live with a direct connection with the Divine where you can receive inner wisdom and love to fill your being with peace, freedom, joy, harmony, purpose, and wisdom? Would you like to have the Divine as a co-creative partner or be in a state of oneness with it for your good as well as all others? Would you like to contribute to a major shift in the evolution of awareness, where peace, love, tolerance, and a higher wisdom fill hearts with good-for-All intentions and actions? Is the world ending or shifting into a higher spiritual consciousness? Would you like to know a higher purpose for your life? Would you like to be filled with love and have your relationships based on it? If your answer is yes to any of these questions, this book is for you.

Have you had an experience where a subtle nudge from within gave you the inner wisdom needed to resolve a difficult situation? If you have, even if you didn't realize it at the time, this was guidance from your divine partner, empowering your life with love and wisdom. LoveAge-creating initiates loving intentions, which allows your divine partner to guide you through difficulties to find solutions of love. The Divine is present 24/7 in order to help you receive what you want to be, to do, or to have.

***

This all-knowing partner helped me continue writing this book at a time when I seriously thought about giving up. After about seven years of writing, I threw out my original manuscript, restructured the book many times, and edited chapters more times than a porcupine has quills. I had actually rewritten one chapter 209 times. Unfortunately, the book still read like a lifeless, sterile technical report that was painfully similar to the ones I wrote as a doctoral candidate at the University of Pittsburgh or as a professor at Westminster College. With a mindset of academic rationality, not to mention being dyslexic, I found it was difficult to write for

Introduction

the general public. It was especially difficult to write from the heart.

I wondered if I would ever learn to write so love would flow from the book's pages. At one point in writing this book, I asked myself, *Why not stop trying to write and just enjoy my retirement instead?* To my surprise, what started out as a highly negative and frustrating writing experience eventually helped me learn more about using divine guidance to receive a deeper understanding of how to express myself with love.

One day, while writing, I felt frustrated. I decided to move from my desk to the recliner where I meditated. I wanted to bring my emotions back into balance, to feel inner calmness and to receive guidance. After a few minutes, a subtle telepathic impression gently settled into my consciousness, "Go to the bookstore to find a book on how to write."

That's all I received. I thought, *What kind of guidance was that? Was the message for real, or was it just a stray thought running through my mind?* I had learned from previous experiences that if I didn't listen to my inner feelings and messages, I would usually live to regret it. I thought, *What harm would it be if I went to the local bookstore here in Buffalo? Besides, I wanted to take a walk to get away from this depressing study.*

While looking through the books at the bookstore, the title, *If You Want to Write,* by Brenda Ueland, caught my attention. It was the subtitle, *A Book about Art, Independence and Spirit* that really piqued my interest. I wondered what she had to say about spirit and writing.

When I looked through the first few pages and saw that the book was published in 1938, I wondered how a book originally published in the year I was born could help in today's publishing environment. I then turned to the back cover and read, "Her best-selling classic on the process of writing that has already inspired thousands to find their own creative center." Since I wanted to find my creative center, I continued reading. It said, "She writes with love and enthusiasm, in a direct, simple, passionate and true way." *That's exactly how I want to write*, I thought.

As I read these words, I became aware of a Beatles' song playing on the bookstore's audio system. It was, *"All You Need Is Love."* I thought, *There goes that song again. It served to give me two other messages from the Divine, and each time it helped clarify questions about incorporating love into my life and book.* I wondered if this was another message of guidance.

I thought, *Either this song was directing me to buy the book, or the source of my inner guidance was a die-hard Beatles fan.* I eventually decided that the song was a personal message from the Divine, and I bought the book.

Once I arrived home, I was anxious to read it. I knew from experience that messages from the Divine always had my well-being at heart, and I was learning more and more to trust them. I had had many of these experiences before, and I am still amazed how they arrived unexpectedly and at the exact time I needed them. This was what Carl Jung, the psychologist, meant by synchronicity and it was how my relationship with the Divine sometimes works. This is an example of one of the ways the Divine directly communicated with me to provide miracles that changed my daily life.

***

I was deeply influenced by what Ueland's book had to say about writing from her creative center, where words and ideas flowed from within. I felt this would probably help me learn to use and trust my own inner source of divine wisdom for writing.

The creative center Ueland spoke about was a source I had known, but I hadn't used it for writing since I felt more comfortable using my rational mind. Unfortunately, using the rational mind restricted the inner flow of love like leaves clogging a roof's gutter. I had to clear out the rational leaves from my mind's gutters and trust the thoughts, feelings, and love flowing from within. If I did, love and wisdom would flow into the book's pages. It was ironic that I was writing about the importance of trusting the inner source of guidance, but I wasn't completely opening my heart at that point to use its guidance while writing.

Eventually, I realized another important aspect about writing. In the beginning, I had thought that all I had to do was to write about love when I should have been *writing with love*. I wanted my pages to resonate with this inner voice of love.

I've always found that it's easier to learn lessons from my own or from others' life experiences than from someone trying to tell me something. When I'm told something, I might learn a little. When I have an experience or read about someone's experiences, they are easier to understand, and it's easier to remember the spiritual principles.

I will therefore share as many of my experiences as possible to help you understand the importance of living with love. They will include some of the irrational things I've done as well as some of my more successful experiences. For me, a mental picture of an experience is worth billions of words, and I hope sharing them helps you understand how the spirituality of love can work in your own daily life. If you haven't noticed yet, I equate creating a life with love with being a spiritual person.

I went through many trial-and-error experiences to learn to be spiritual. The five shifts evolved mainly from my own personal experiences of hard knocks and pain. It has been said that a wise person learns from his or her mistakes as well as from others. I'm sure you'll see your own life experiences in some of mine—hopefully the better ones. It is my hope that by sharing the lessons I learned, I can help you learn to create with the power of love more quickly and with less pain and struggle than I had.

While this book is based on my personal spiritual development of learning to live with love, it isn't a chronological listing of significant events or turning points from birth to now. Instead, the five shifts in consciousness provided the structure for the book's contents.

Another area that will be discussed is about earth's possible destruction. Are humans or natural disasters going to destroy us, or are we going to change our consciousness to bring love and harmony into personal and collective relationships? I believe the latter has a higher probability of occurring, and a significant evolutionary change in consciousness is already happening. However, the likelihood of it happening increases as each additional person accepts and practices the way of love.

Biological evolution was primarily a reaction to a changing environment, but today humans are in charge of their destiny. We have the freedom to consciously choose the age of love, it will not happen automatically. Do you want to be part of an evolutionary change of consciousness that is shifting from the ego to Love Age enlightenment that will help bring peace and love to our planet? If so, choose it. During the 15 year process of writing this book, I learned that helping to create the Love Age was to become my life's purpose. I hope it will be yours too.

What is your life's purpose???

When I started writing this book, I wanted to share it only with members of my former religion. After writing for some years, I began to realize that the book should be written for a worldwide audience. I began to realize that there was a major evolutionary change in consciousness happening, and it involved the principles of love I was writing about. Instead of wanting to share my experiences just with

Introduction

those in my former religion, I wanted to help contribute to the shift in consciousness of the Love Age.

If you want to be a part of this, do not merely read this book, but also put it into practice. The US Army once had a slogan, "An Army of One." You, instead, can be a "Love Age pioneer of One" or a "Love Age creator of One." One person at a time will co-create the age of love by changing his or her ego consciousness into the practice of living and creating a life with divine love. The world desperately depends on you. That is how important you are for the evolution of your own life's consciousness and that of the world.

Being religious or nonreligious doesn't matter. If you have problems with words like God, Spirit, or other spiritual words, please substitute Universe, Universal Wisdom, Source, Universal Source or Force, Energy, or other words acceptable to you. Words are only symbolic pointers to something, and are not the real thing, so don't allow a reaction to words stop you from reading or accepting spiritual principles. I use Divine Source, Loving Source, or the Divine to refer to God, while different religions use other names. See the first chapter, where I go into this issue of names in more detail.

Being spiritual is not the same as being religious. People on an institutionalized religious path, who submit to the authority of their religion and have blind faith in its dogmas, rituals, myths, worship services, sacred books, and leaders, are not being spiritual. If a person has a partnership and a direct relationship with the Divine's love and wisdom, that person is spiritual. Many people in the mystical branches of religions have this relationship. However, being a practicing member of a religion does not exclude one from being spiritual. But that person would need to be less influenced by institutional practices and would need to live a more direct and personal relationship of love with the

Your Creative Power of Love

Divine.

The fastest growing spiritual group in America comprises those who do not belong to a religion and who simply identify themselves as spiritual. Those who were raised by parents who were not religious like mine have become increasingly disillusioned with the secular life. They don't like religious organizations, but they feel more comfortable with being spiritual. I currently do not belong to any established religion and prefer to call myself spiritual.

You, as a divine being, are pure love. Just know your true essence is love and use the creative power of this love to transform your personal life. All else will take care of itself.

Have you taken one small step today to be more loving???

SHIFT I

Ego Self to a Divine Self

Who am I? Humans have been seeking an answer to this question for ages. Most people believe themselves to be the body/ego self, which consists of the body and aspects of the mind, subconscious mind, social culture, and emotions of fear that make up the ego. This is what people usually refer to when they use the words "I" or "me." Families, religions, science, and other social institutions strongly influence how you define the ego self, while spiritual people experience a different identity of who they are. Humans are divine beings; therefore the Divine Self needs to be placed in charge of the ego self. In order for the Love Age to evolve, the consciousness of the world must transition from the ego identity to the Divine Self. The world is in need of this paradigm shift. This is the only way individuals and societies can consciously infuse divine love, wisdom, and good-for-all solutions into their lives for creating a better world. I made this shift in identity, which I would like to share with you.

Chapter One

Paradigm Shift to a Divine Self

Mary's father waited in his car to pick up his daughter at kindergarten. It was a rainy day, and Mary was dressed in a pink raincoat with a matching umbrella. He noticed that she was trying to tiptoe around water puddles. When she eventually reached the car, he buckled her into the child's seat as quickly as he could and noticed she was frowning.

"What's wrong, honey? Is the strap too tight?"

"No, Daddy. I just don't want to be a shoe any more. They get too dirty and wet."

"What do you mean you don't want to be a shoe?"

"You're the one who told me I'm a shoe."

"When did I say you were a shoe?"

"Didn't you tell me to say, 'I'm sole?' I don't want to be the bottom of a shoe anymore."

***

Most people are as confused as Mary about who they are. Those who cannot see beyond the body and ego self will often react like Mary, by diminishing the self's identity to something physical or mental. I lived that illusion for 35 years or more before I realized the ego wasn't my true self. The Divine Self or Soul is the true self, and it should be in charge and collaborating with the ego self.

We need to transition into a more cooperative, peaceful, and loving consciousness, or we may realize our worst destiny. In order for you to be spiritual, you must make an identity paradigm shift. Instead of the ego, the Divine Self and its love and wisdom should be consciously guiding your intentions and actions.

The ego's negative values and habits must cease to control the Divine Self and the ego should assume a supportive status instead. The ego's unproductive reactions and habits need to be recognized, taken responsibility for, and replaced. These are the three-Rs for initiating and placing the Divine Self in charge: *Recognize it* (ego habit). *Responsible for it. Replace it.* Making this shift in consciousness is needed in order to initiate the habits of love, peace, joy, and freedom.

Do You Have More than One Self?

Before I attended church as a teenager, I thought I only had one self. After becoming familiar with the concept of soul as a Christian, I became aware that I might be more than one self. While on Earth, it seemed that I had a soul floating around in heaven, and when I died, I would become it. I understood I was the ego self while living on Earth, and I would become soul once I passed on.

When I was in college and read about early Quakers, they practiced silent group meditations in order to experience the profound peace of the "Inner Light." It was my first introduction to going within to find the presence of the Divine Self.

Paradigm Shift to a Divine Self

While I was a Quaker, I tried Transcendental Meditation, since it proclaimed itself as a way to find inner peace. I didn't remain in the group very long since the meditation wasn't effective for me. In addition, I was told that I had a personal mantra, but the same mantra was given to other followers too.

In the late 1960s, I made a discovery that shattered the illusion of only being an ego self with a soul in Heaven. During this time, my wife was also exploring spiritual frontiers, and she introduced me to Edgar Cayce. Cayce would go within to channel medical and other spiritual wisdom, and I wanted to be able to tap into that source of inner wisdom too.

Cayce also helped me accept the idea of reincarnation. According to reincarnation, I had two selves, a divine soul and an earthly ego self. The earthly physical or ego self was temporary for a given life, until the body died, but the real self, Soul, was eternal and reincarnated in new bodies, life after life. I also learned that *karma,* derived from past life ego motivations and actions, was carried with me life after life until I learned the lessons of love.

After Cayce, my next introduction to Soul was in Eckankar™ where I learned I was Soul now and could use it to travel into inner spiritual dimensions. I didn't have to wait till I died to experience Soul or the spiritual worlds, since I could project myself there now. I learned I was already my Divine Self, my true identity. I was also not limited to an earthly self that existed only in physical and mental forms. In addition, I was Soul now, with spiritual awareness and powers. I was a divine being or Soul, and it was this higher self that should be in charge of the ego self. I'm still working to place Soul in total charge.

We Are Fraternal Twins with an Ego Self & a Divine Self

The Divine, Soul, and Subtle Energy Fields

To understand who we are as Soul, it is necessary to know the relationship between the body/ego self, the subtle energy fields, Soul, and the Divine. Soul (Divine Self) is the bridge that allows Divine Energy to enter the subtle energy bodies (i.e., mental, memory, intuition, and emotional energy fields). When I use the word "Divine," I am referring to the Divine Self as well as to the Divine Source and to Divine Energy. The Divine is a trinity.

Figure 1.1 represents the three as Divine Source, Divine Energy, and Divine Self that are pure divine love. They also serve to channel love, wisdom, and creative energy into the subtle energy bodies and physical body for the purpose of creating, healing, as well as maintaining life. The Divine is within and surrounds you and is everywhere. It is not an upper external layer, as depicted in the illustration. The picture uses earthly space and time, but in reality, there is no up or down, single location, beginning, ending, space, or time when it comes to the Divine Source, Divine Energy, or Divine Self.

The hearts with sparkling halos flowing from the Divine Source represent divine love. When you are a clear channel for this love, it affects thoughts, memories, emotions, the physical body, the physical environment, and social life. When the ego does not block the divine flow, the Divine Self is energized to create with love.

Divine Source

Figure 1.1 serves to show how divine love flows into your life when the Divine Self is in control as opposed to the ego self. The word, Divine Source is what most religions usually refer to as God. I also refer to the Divine Source as the Loving Source. The Divine Source is also called the unmanifested, the One, the All, Allah, Jehovah, Brahma, Krishna, and other names.

Figure 1.1

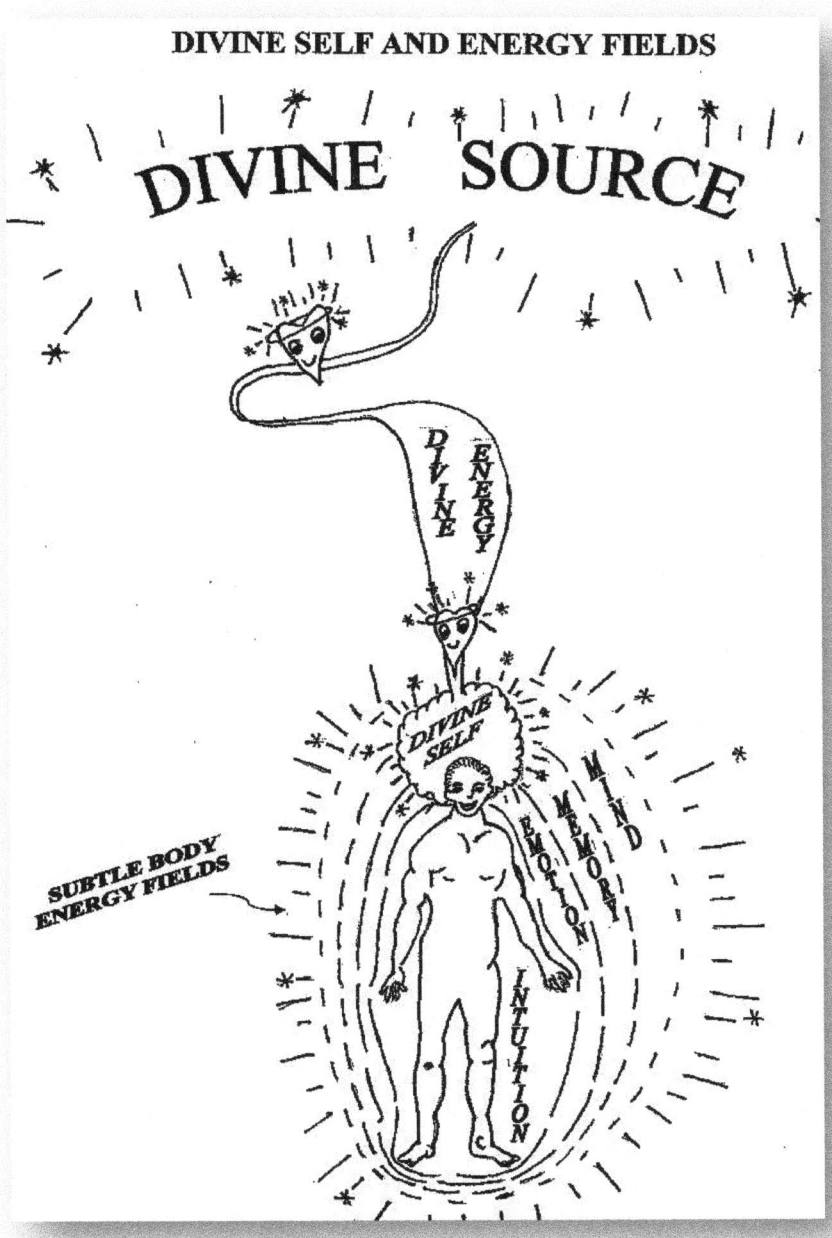

These are only symbolic names pointing to the real thing. The name "God" and its connotation of wrath carries a lot of negative baggage since it justifies violence, prejudice, inequality, gender and sexual bias, and other unloving acts. I therefore prefer to use a more neutral word. The name is not what is important, since it is only a word pointing to the real Divine. What is most important is experiencing the Divine rather than what name it's given. Even children have their own ideas about God's name.

***

Johnny and Chris were arguing on the playground during recess about the name of God. Johnny said, "His name is Harold."

Chris said, "No sir, His name is Andy! Where did you ever get the name Harold?"

"When we pray the Lord's Prayer, don't we say? 'Our father in heaven. Harold be your name...?' See, Harold's his name."

"You're not saying it right. Besides, in the song, 'He Walks with Me' that we sing in church, we sing, 'An-dy walks with me; An-dy talks with me...' See? His name is Andy."

For those who are not familiar with Christian practices, the Lord's Prayer is supposed to read, "Our father in heaven. *Hallowed* be your name..." The song, "He Walks with Me," is supposed to have the lyrics, "*And he* walks with me; *And he* talks with me..." Does this help?

***

The Divine has no male or female gender. I use the pronoun *It* most of the time, when referring to the Divine Source. This is about the best pronoun available in the English language to refer to something without giving it a gender bias. Our language is so ego biased toward gender identity that it does not have a pronoun referring to neutral gender beings that exist in spiritual forms or dimensions. Also, as the Divine Self or Soul you are neither male nor female.

The Divine Source is the starting place from which all love, wisdom, life, unmanifested energy, healing energy, and all else derives in order to manifest forms in the material and spiritual worlds. It's the source of all unmanifested energy, which becomes manifested forms or material on Earth. Unmanifested creative energy at the subatomic level is what makes all things in the universe exist. When affected by divine consciousness or the thoughts of humans, it manifests as material forms that we see in the outer world.

Divine Energy

Divine Energy flows from the Divine Source and carries all of the divine goodies like love and wisdom with it. Religions refer to the Divine Energy as Holy Spirit, Life Force, *Chi*, *Reiki*, or spirit, to name a few. Quantum scientists who theorize string theory refer to it as "strings."

The essence of divine love, wisdom, and creative energy derives from the Divine Source in the form of Divine Energy. These inner divine attributes flow through Soul as a passageway to enter the subtle energy fields, the body, and the material world. Divine Energy is what you experience as love, divine wisdom, light, sound, houses, cars, body, and other energy forms. It is in every atom of the spiritual and material worlds of form.

As the Divine Energy moves from the Divine Source into the world of matter, its vibrations progressively become lower. The first reduction of Divine Energy from unmanifested energy is observed in the form of sound and light vibrations. This is why those who have near death experiences or who experience divine presence usually see lights or light beings, and hear the sounds of the spiritual worlds.

Divine Self

You and I are Divine Energy individualized as the Divine Self or Soul, which makes us divine beings with expanded awareness. Divine Self has the power of awareness by which it can observe what is going on in the spiritual dimensions, in subtle energy bodies (mental and emotional), in the physical body, in the physical world, and in social environments.

Since the Divine Self evolved from Divine Energy, it is embodied with divine love, wisdom, and creative energy. Divine Self has the power to direct attention and to connect us with the energies of love and wisdom in order to co-create matter and circumstance. The Divine Self also has the power of co-creating for the good-for-All when it is not controlled by the ego and works in harmony with divine love. It can consciously use thoughts, emotions, and imagination to help co-create the world of matter out of the unmanifested energy that flows from the Divine Source. The Divine Self can guide its intentions with divine wisdom and can co-create for the good-of-All.

> *The Divine Self Dwells within Me as the True Me*

This Divine Self is our true identity. It is eternal and never dies as the ego body does. This eternal identity carries past life choices and their consequences from one life to another and is stored within the subtle bodies. The *karma* stored there is what determines much of our experiences and circumstances in life and provides most of the lessons we need to learn.

When there is no ego barrier blocking spirit, you allow love, wisdom, divine guidance, and creative powers to flow freely into you and through you. This places Soul in charge as a benevolent being producing peace, freedom, justice, love, and joy in relationships. Without the Divine Self in charge, the ego remains in control, and you suffer the consequences of its unconscious and unproductive habits.

With Soul in Charge, Creating Is for the Good-of-All

I had to find ways to place Soul in charge by replacing ego habits with spiritual habits of love. Once the subconscious mind and emotions learned spiritual habits, it was easier for Soul to respond and to live in harmony with the divine's purpose.

The essence of the Divine Self is love. Therefore, I'm love. I'm still working on realizing my true essence as being love and on just being love in every aspect of my life.

My desired relationship with the Divine is to have Soul in charge, to be the Divine's co-creative partner, and eventually to live in oneness with it. This isn't the easiest task to do, which is why it is still a work in progress. Since life is a dance of balance between the inner and outer, the Divine Self must be the lead dancer to guide life's dances. This allows you to live in harmony with what's good-for-All.

Is Soul or the Divine the lead partner in your life's dance?

To summarize, the *Divine Source* is like the electrical power plant that produces the electricity (i.e., unmanifested energy, divine love, wisdom, creative energy, and life force). *Divine Energy* serves as the power line that carries all of the essence or transmissions flowing from the electrical generating plant of the Divine Source to the world and to us.

Electricity has to be reduced in power by transformers in order to be useful in homes, a process that is similar to the stepping down of Divine Energy to make it useful in the inner worlds and in our earthly existence. The *Divine Self* as well as our *chakras*, which will be discussed in a later chapter, serve a similar function to that of a transformer that lowers electrical power to run refrigerators, dishwashers, and other useful electrical appliances.

Soul, thoughts, intentions, feelings, and imagination help to convert unmanifested energy into manifested energy for useful purposes when we are in a co-creative or oneness relationship with the Divine and with others. Divine Self serves as a channel of love to allow the life force or Divine Energy to manifest life, to animate and maintain the body, and to perform other biological, social, and spiritual functions.

Unfortunately, the ego is like a terrorist blowing up the electrical power lines of wisdom and love that flow into Soul and the home of the self. When this happens, disharmony, unhappiness, and other ego consequences happen, until its destructive presence is recognized.

We need to be the electrical worker who goes out during an ego storm and who recognizes ego's unconscious reactions and habits in order to reconnect our homes to the power lines of love and wisdom. This is what living and creating with love and what being a spiritual person does.

To create with love, you must shift your identity from the ego self to the Divine Self. Doing so will make personal relationships more loving and peaceful. In the next chapter, the recognition of the ego terrorist will be examined.

Figure 1.2

> **SUGGESTED QUESTIONS FOR PERSONAL AND GROUP DISCUSSION**
> 1. How do you answer the question, "Who am I?"
> 2. Do you now view your true self as soul or the Divine Self?
> 3. How do you create the things you want in your life?
> 4. What word do you use to refer to the Divine (e.g., he, she, it, mother/father, etc.)?
> 5. Do you view the relationships between the body, energy fields, and the Divine differently than depicted in Figure 1.1?
> 6. Do you believe your true self is the Divine Self or Soul?
> 7. Have you experienced the divine love and wisdom of Divine Energy?
> 8. Have you experienced the inner light or sound of Divine Energy?
> 9. Have you experienced Soul being the conscious observer of your ego habits?

☺ *Smile* ☺
Your true self, rather than being the ego terrorist, is a divine being with spiritual powers of love.

Chapter Two

Recognizing the Ego

If asked the question, *Who am I*, most would identify with their bodies, minds, or emotions, or with how their cultural values, beliefs, and roles define them. These are the elements of the ego self, or what some may refer to as the "I" or as "my personality." This is the primary way humans identify, separate, and distinguish themselves from others.

Egos are unconscious mental constructions derived mainly from social institutions and cultures. The ego is not a solid piece of reality that exists or stands alone by itself. Instead, it is mainly a mental illusion that is socially constructed and maintained by the family, education, government, economy, and religion of the society we are born into and live in. The ego is primarily the "institutional me."

The family is a powerful determiner of the ego consciousness, since it often determines our nationality, culture, religion, political party, economic class, beliefs, and educational opportunities. To a great extent, the family defines the ego's identity, since it determines our social roles, whether we are religious or secular or of a higher or lower social status, and more. For example, the subordinate status of women in Muslim cultures is to a great extent determined by the family and religion.

Some people do not accept the ego definitions their society defines for them. A spiritual person is one who does not accept the ego consciousness of his or her society. Individually, we have the freedom to choose what we want to be and to choose our own identity, beliefs, roles, and values. Today's youth are doing this more and more frequently than in past generations, and the women's movement is also gaining more worldwide influence.

Ego Identity is a Mentally Constructed Illusion by Society

When I was a teenager, the church constructed my faith-based ego, and I wasn't aware that it was being done. I had decided on my own to attend church because I felt an inner emptiness stemming from my parents' lack of religion. For some reason, I thought attending church would eliminate my feelings of emptiness.

I accepted most of the church's beliefs on faith, especially the belief in the Bible being the infallible word of God. Since the Bible was the record of God's communication, I strongly believed it to be true and rejected anything that suggested otherwise. Either I had faith in it, or I didn't. It was a black or white issue with no middle ground that allowed questioning the interpretation of the Bible I was given. Conforming to my religion's interpretation of the Bible built my ego's faith-based self.

***

When I later attended West Virginia Wesleyan College to become a Methodist minister, I attended a New Testament Bible class taught by Dr. Teeple. He was a biblical scholar who had researched the Bible in its original text. He valued evidence-based knowledge above church dogma and was an impressive scholar.

Recognizing the Ego

Fortunately for me, he presented an interpretation of the Bible that was different from my own beliefs. He was familiar with how the Bible changed over time in order to agree with the beliefs of those in charge of cultural values. The Bible actually incorporated the ego cultural beliefs of its time, including the subjection of women to a second-class citizenship. This was not what Jesus taught nor what he practiced, since women were included as part of the early Christian leadership. Dr. Teeple taught me that the Bible was not the infallible word of God as I thought it was.

I learned the New Testament was written 60 to 100 years after Christ's death and that it was based on secondhand stories passed from one person to another before they were written down. Can you imagine what would happen to the story of your life if we waited 60 to 100 years after your death to record it? The professor also told us that the spiritually inspired writers of the New Testament's four gospels were affected by the culture of their times and that they used different sources to compile their accounts of Jesus's life. The gospel writers of Matthew and Luke used the gospel of Mark and a "Q" source. In addition, the Bible had gone through various translations and interpretations, where passages were changed to agree with later cultural or religious beliefs. This was all in direct conflict with what I believed, and at first, I refused to believe what he was teaching about the Bible. My ego-based faith in the Bible was being challenged, and my ego reacted to protect itself, in the same way as others in my class reacted.

During a college event where students could invite parents to attend classes, some of the students brought family members to the New Testament class. One of the students who believed as I did decided to criticize the professor for teaching lies about the Bible. She probably gained the courage to say what she did since her parents were present.

She said, "The Bible is the written word of God and not written by men. If you teach such a thing, you'll go to hell."

Her attack had emotionally shaken the professor. He did his best to dispute her deeply hurting ego reaction. I felt sorry for him. He was an honest, gentle, truthful, and good man, as I saw from what limited perceptions I picked up from classroom contact. I knew he was deeply concerned about his students and that he bent over backward to help us understand his truth about the Bible. I didn't think it was fair for the student to say what she did, even though I agreed with her blind faith in the Bible. My reactions to protect the ego were kept internal, unlike her scathing vocal condemnation of the professor.

I listened to the professor during the rest of the semester, and much of what he said made sense, but I still didn't want to step outside my faith in the Bible. My blind faith and ego attachments to what the church taught limited my freedom to choose or even to consider new information based on objective observations. I reacted to any challenges to my faith-based ego, but these reactions softened over time.

Being confused for almost two years, I went back and forth in my beliefs, until eventually I decided that the professor was right. I stepped outside my blind faith in the Bible and the fundamentalists' interpretation of Jesus's life. My belief in the Bible had been the basis of my religious faith, and when that went, it opened doors to questioning other ego-based institutional beliefs. The vanishing of that faith also helped to redefine who I was as well as my beliefs.

***

Little did I know, when I was a church member, that I was taught an interpretation of Jesus's life rather than his actual teachings. What I learned was mainly the dogma and myths that grew up around Jesus's life, which were added to the Bible or were the church's interpretation of what Jesus taught. Scholars have concluded that it's difficult to know the historical Jesus.

Even the early Christian church had three major interpretations of Jesus's teachings. James viewed them as a part of Judaism and St. Paul's interpretation became the Orthodox

Church that opened Christianity to gentiles, while the *Gnostics*, a more mystical group, were targeted for elimination by the Orthodox Church. Much of Christianity was a mental construction of the dogmas and myths of the orthodox group, which made it an ego-based institution, as many religions are today.

These events constituted the first time I realized that social institutions helped construct my mental ego beliefs. I didn't think of these beliefs as being my ego at that time, but all of this was part of how I interpreted myself as having a fundamentalist or evangelical Christian identity. Beliefs, dogmas, and myths of religion and of other institutions were often the bars constructing my ego's prison. Recognizing my ego habits that derived from social institutions was the first step in helping me change them.

> ***Must Recognize Ego Habits to Change Them***

My New Testament professor was only at the college for two or three years. As I look back on this experience, I'm thankful the Divine brought him into my life to help move me to a higher understanding based on evidence, which served as a guiding light for my spiritual quest.

The Divine often brought people like the professor into my life. Earlier, a student minister at my church had encouraged me to attend Bethany College where he attended. Before that, I planned to be a coal miner like my father, but the mines had laid off workers and were not hiring. I had to find something else to do.

I believed my minister was divinely placed in my life at that exact time to encourage me to attend Bethany College, which I was not academically prepared to do. Consequently, I did not have the grades to continue there as a student.

The Divine was always using others to help me on my spiritual journey and guided me when my heart and spiritual eyes were not open enough to see where I should direct my life. These gentle encouragements from people as well as feelings of emptiness were often the way the Divine guided me, early in my spiritual unfoldment. When I later realized how the Divine operated and how it guided me, I realized that life was indeed purposeful.

Ego self is dogma-based, while the Divine Self is evidence-based. During my sophomore year in college, I decided to major in sociology, which was a discipline based on scientific or evidence-based information about how society and groups affect behavior. Along with the New Testament class, it helped me make the transition from a fundamentalist to a liberal/social Christian as well as to make other changes in my life. The study of social institutions showed me how groups helped construct the ego consciousness via religious, political, educational, economic, and family values and beliefs through the process of socialization. I also thought sociology, based on scientific evidence, would help me know how to change institutions to make the world more peaceful and just. These academic influences helped transform my identity from a faith-based ego to one that relied more on evidence-based information.

I also became a believer in nonviolence as a way to change society. I was disturbed with the Methodists and with other churches for not realizing that Jesus taught love and nonviolence, which they chose to ignore. Instead, the church was justifying intolerance, injustices, and wars. I consequently decided to become a Quaker in order to focus my attention on the use of nonviolence for changing governments of the world to be more peaceful and just. I didn't realize it at the time, but my personal life and society's collective ego consciousness were based on conflict, which was the major reason the world was a warring and violent place. I wanted to help reconstruct those mental ego beliefs of warring governments in order to transform them into instruments of peace.

Mind and Institutions Construct Ego's Realities

The Ego Is a Victim and Lives for the Good-of-me

When the ego consciousness rules life, it engages in good-for-me conflicts with others in order to maximize its selfish needs. It creates the hell-like circumstances that most people unconsciously live in, and it is unfortunately the prevailing consciousness of humankind. It's what you see daily in your relationships with others and in the relationships between nations.

Egos Are Always Me-deep into Themselves

The ego consciousness not only motivates the lives of individuals, but it also runs our ego-based institutions. When the ego consciousness runs social institutions, it also creates social disharmony, stress, greed, suffering, and unhappiness at the personal and community levels. *The ego self is greed-based and conflict-based.*

Have you noticed that conflicts exist in most families, and their conflicts can create family discord, divorces, or even violence? The conflicts and polarizations between political parties in the United States have made it very difficult for the country to make the needed decisions to move us forward for the greater good. The greediness of corporations and of Wall Street serves the greedy rich and has brought the economy to the brink of economic collapse, but they still resist reform. The educational system focuses mainly on the mind and is deeply imbedded in the ego consciousness of rationalism and dogmatic science. Religions fight with each other and amongst themselves, as well as with secular science and cultures. Religion is used to justify wars; practitioners will die for it and will do anything except practice the love that most religions teach. We are living in the Ego Age of increasing polarization and conflicts.

The ego consciousness has now arrived at an evolutionary endpoint where conflict and disharmony are no longer serving *Homo sapiens*. The ego desire for survival and the use of fear used to serve humans in its early existence. With the increased destructive power that technology has placed in our hands, the old ego values of conflict, intolerance, greed, unconscious thinking, and fears have created a very dangerous and unhappy world.

Ego Is Addicted to Greed, Conflict, and Unhappiness

I believe it was Aldous Huxley who said that it just might be possible that this world is another planet's hell. We may already be living the hell some had hoped to escape after death. William Sunday said, "If there is no hell, a good many preachers are obtaining money under false pretenses." Maybe they are just not clear about where or what hell is. Could it be the ego consciousness within us?

Ego Complaining and Victim Consciousness

When I was a child, my parents were the primary influences affecting my beliefs and behaviors. Parents develop primary ego patterns for relating to their children and to each other. My father was the one in control of family money and decisions. His main ego method of gaining control was to complain. My mother, on the other hand, responded with the victim consciousness of "poor me" and wanted her children's sympathy so we would side with her and be against my father. I primarily adopted my father's habit of complaining but also used the victim consciousness to control others.

Recognizing the Ego

***

It wasn't until I was a freshman at West Virginia Wesleyan College that I began to become aware of how I used my mother's victim consciousness. When I met my friends on campus, they would often ask, "How are you doing?" This was a great opener for my victim consciousness to rise to its glory and tell them how bad my life was and to hope they would feel sorry for poor me.

I noticed after a while they would try to avoid me, and I began to wonder why. When I exchanged greetings, I began to notice their negative reactions to my complaining about the weather or about the burden of being a student. I wanted them to feel sorry for me, but they didn't.

Later, after I realized I was using the same victim response my mother used, I no longer wanted to be a victim seeking sympathy from others. If I was going to change this ego habit, I had to recognize when I used it and to be aware of the disharmony it created. I gradually recognized how I used it to manipulate the sympathy of my fellow classmates, and I started to tone it down. Unfortunately, using the victim response was still a habit when I was later married, but it was not as pervasive as my complaining. My wife and later my children would usually bring it to my attention when I unconsciously used the "poor me" victim consciousness.

In my relationship with my wife, I took on the complaining ego role especially when disagreements arose about finances, while she in turn poured on the guilt. I was completely unaware that our relationship had a complaining/guilt habit that made our egos react, which caused disharmony in the family.

It took me much longer to recognize the ego habit of complaining was also an extension of the "poor me" victim habit. Complainers view themselves as victims. I was in an ego prison, and some of the bars were made out of the complaints about being a poor victim of my wife's spending habits. Since I felt complaining gave me power and control, it took me many years to recognize how its bars imprisoned me.

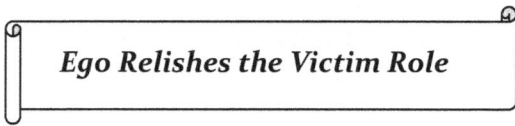
Ego Relishes the Victim Role

What main ego habit creates most of the bars of your ego prison?

***

How many egos does it take to screw in a light bulb? Actually, none. It is below their me-centeredness and overinflated ego superiority to do maintenance work. They would gladly sit in the dark, complaining and arguing that someone else should change it. Such is the nature of the ego.

Recognizing the Complaining Ego

It took about 35 years of marriage before I became aware of the complaining/guilt relationship I had with my wife, Audrey. The ego response usually started with my projecting the next month's bills and realizing either we would not have enough money or it was too close to call. This would create fears about our financial future, and I would start complaining to my wife.

***

"Just look at next month's budget; we're not going to have enough money, and you're going to have to stop spending so much."

"I'm not the one who spends all the money. You're the one who bought the lawn mower this month."

"What did you expect me to do? I sure wasn't going to go out there and chew the grass off with my teeth. I had to buy the lawn mower. Besides, you said it was all right to buy it. You're the one who's buying clothes and other stuff all the time. Why don't you cut back on that?"

"If you had some wives, they would spend all your money."

"What do other wives have to do with next month's bills? You should be doing something now to cut back on your spending. You're the cause of our budget problems."

"Probably when I die, you'll buy your next wife all the jewelry and clothes she wants, and you'll not say a word to her."

***

Then the argument escalated into a shouting match, and we would both be angry until it got so hot that one of us had to walk away. This ego reacting of back and forth complaints and guilt got us nowhere except to create disharmony in the family. I thought I won, since I pointed out her bad spending habits, and she thought she won by making me feel guilty about mine. At times, I would feel bad, not only because I felt angry that nothing was accomplished, but I felt guilty about the possibility of treating my imagined next wife better than I treated Audrey. Guilt is subtle, but it is also powerful.

Sometime around 1993 or 1994, we became aware of this unconscious ego habit and started to discuss it. Recognition of our unconscious ego habit was the first move toward changing it. When I started to look more deeply into why this ego pattern started in the first place, I realized it was about my fear of financial insecurity of the future. I didn't like future uncertainties, especially financial ones.

When I looked beneath any of my ego reactions, I discovered there was always some type of fear about loss associated with it. I was attached to a secure financial future and feared the possible loss of it. This, then, led to the irrational behavior of blaming my wife for our financial circumstances and I complained in order to try to control what I thought was her unwise buying. Did you notice that the complainer is never at fault, nor is the one using guilt? Each of us was protecting our ego identity by blaming the other one for our financial circumstances.

Threatened Ego Engages in Conflict to Protect Itself

Audrey and I even went to the point of scheduling a short one-day trip to a lake in the mountains to discuss what we were going to do about this ego pattern of relating to each other. I took a pad and pen to record an agreement.

In the agreement, I was to try to catch my ego response of future financial problems before they turned into fears. If I didn't do this and began complaining, Audrey was to point out that I was complaining. I was to stop complaining and to discuss the situation without giving judgments or accusing her. If this did not work, and Audrey started firing her guilt bullets, I was to bring it to her attention that she was using guilt. We hoped this would help each of us recognize how we were responding with ego reactions and would stop the cycle of firing ego bullets back and forth at each other.

Well, I have to confess this approach did not work. If I caught my initial reaction of financial fear and stopped its reactions, it would usually work. If it went beyond that point, which it usually did, we were to remind the other spouse how their ego was reacting. Unfortunately, we returned to our old ego pattern of escalating the argument. It seemed that when the other person pointed out what the ego was doing, the ego would feel threatened and would react to protect itself. We would then fall back into our old reacting pattern of machine-gunning complaints and guilt to gain control over each other.

> ### *Ego or Intellect Without Love is the Enemy Within*

We gradually managed to gain some control over this problem when I decided to adopt my wife's attitude about money. She has a tremendous trust in the Divine that everything will be provided. So she keeps her focus on the present rather than on the future like me. On the other hand, Audrey hates planning anything, especially finances, while I overplan. Life is a balance between trusting the Divine and doing what we need to do in order to make things happen. Some people overplan, as I did, and act without divine guidance or trust, while others rely too much on the Divine, as though it was their free welfare system, without being responsible. Audrey was not that far from the center or balanced state, but I had to give up my overplanning and trust more in the Divine in order to stop the initial ego reaction before it escalated into a conflict.

For my part, I began to have more faith in receiving and trusting in the Divine by turning over problems to it. Now, my wife does the finances and plans for the current month, while I wait for a financial disaster to happen. I hope you realize I'm just kidding about the last comment—or am I?

When the ego self is devoid of love and trust in the Divine, it becomes the enemy within, and this is the consciousness that we all need to change. Instead of operating my personal life with ego-based decisions and solutions, I had to replace them with love-based ones.

This was the first time I consciously recognized an ego pattern in my marriage and consciously did something about it. I learned that the ego and its negative reactions that caused disharmony was the true enemy of love flowing from within. Even though the ego is the enemy within, we are still responsible for loving it. Didn't Jesus say, "Love your enemies?" Hating the ego is reacting to it, which means that it will continue to keep you in its

Your Creative Power of Love

grip. Loving and not reacting to it will free you. When you love the ego, please do not identify with it.

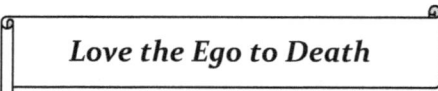

Love the Ego to Death

Changing my attitude and behavior about financial insecurity helped to minimize the ego's reactions, but I learned never to count out fear, since it will raise its ego head when and where I least expect it. I had to keep vigilance over my reactions and the fears that caused them. This will be the topic of the next chapter, and it is probably an issue that I will have to address for the rest of my life.

Can you name one ego habit that creates disharmony in your relationships???

Figure 2.1

SUGGESTED QUESTIONS FOR PERSONAL AND GROUP DISCUSSION

1. Is the ego consciousness responsible for creating the hell-like circumstances here on Earth?
2. How does your ego consciousness filter how you perceive reality?
3. Have you ever used the victim consciousness to get others to feel sorry for you?
4. What social institutions have you noticed using ego-based consciousness?
5. Have you ever tried stopping an ego pattern that you used when relating to others?
6. Have you ever tried to protect your ego from attack? If so, what reaction (anger, gossip, guilt, complaining, etc.) did you use?
7. Are you mostly unconscious or conscious of how the ego operates in your life?

Chapter Three

Ego is Fear-based

Meister Eckhart, a thirteenth-century Catholic theologian, teacher, and mystic, believed that at the heart of one's spiritual life is the problem of attachment to things, people, beliefs, and other earthly things. He said, "To be full of things is to be empty of God. To be empty of things is to be full of God." At another time he said, "He who would be serene and pure needs but one thing, detachment."

Although Meister Eckhart did not use the word "ego," the main function of the ego is to be attached to whatever it deems important for the good-of-me. If you are attached to things, there is a fear of losing them. *The ego is attachment-based.*

The way to rid yourself of a fear is to be detached from losing it. Since attachments are like mental glue, the way to dissolve the bond is not to place so much importance on things or circumstances. If you desire an automobile, a good relationship, or success, accept and be grateful for what you already have, and do not let the worry or fear of not receiving it or of its loss make you miserable. Hold a balanced emotion where you are neither overly joyful about receiving it nor worried about its potential loss. Detach the mental glue.

> ### *Fears & Worries Are Paying High Interest on Something You Rarely Receive or Lose*

In Eastern religions, detachment is an important belief and practice. Detachment is easy to understand mentally, but it is difficult to practice. Since beliefs and status things define the ego, it does not want to give up these attachments. If I have lots of things, I'm a rich ego. If I lose my things, I'm a poor victimized ego producing a great deal of fear. The bond between things and the identity of being rich is held together by the ego's super glue.

There are two primary motivators in life—fear and love, and the ego thrives on fear. Since the ego is built on mental attachments, it is controlled by the fear of losing them. Fears become powerful negative thoughts that energize emotions and serve as a motivation for directing life in irrational and conflicting ways. This is not a harmonious or peaceful way to live.

> ### *Fears Arise from Attachments*

My first step in changing an ego habit was to recognize it (e.g., my complaining), then to recognize the underlying fear that energized it (e.g., fear of the lack of money in the future), and finally to detach mentally from the fear. To help you recognize some of the underlying fears of the ego, I am going to list them, explain them, and give some examples. However, this will not be an exhaustive list of fears.

Fear of Abandonment

The fear of abandonment is one of my wife's predominant fears. She lost her father when she was eleven months old and lost her mother when she was in eighth grade. I feel certain that she had experiences of being abandoned in past lives, since it seems to be one of her main lessons to learn for this lifetime. Fear of abandonment is associated with the fear of being alone or losing loved ones.

When Audrey goes to the grocery store or shopping, she always wants someone to be with her. When we are in Minnesota during the summertime, she is lonely for her children and grandchildren in California and wants to return. If I would die before her, she would most likely move in with our youngest daughter the next day, or close to it.

Where there is fear of abandonment, it is difficult to trust those who are close to you. There is always an underlying fear that they will abandon you. Some have a haunting fear of losing someone in their family to an accident, illness, or divorce, or through moving away from friends, or through some other form of mini-death. This fear is mainly rooted in an attachment to people and fearing the possible loss of them.

Fear of Losing Ego's Status

Since the ego constructs a social status or identity and is attached to it, there is always the fear of losing it. People are like actors, since they rely on external popularity and acceptance but fear its loss. Teens are threatened with the fear of not being accepted by their peers. They are vulnerable to this fear since they are trying to become more independent of their parents and at the same time develop stronger ties with their peers. They will often dress in strange ways or do things to be like their peers that are different from what their parents want them to be or do.

In addition, there is the fear of losing one's sense of self-worth, which is a very fragile thing, since the ego tries to define it by using external approval. Your worth is outside yourself, like the popularity of movie stars, and it is difficult to control. Social achievements are short-lived, which makes self-worth vulnerable. There is also the fear of embarrassment that can put dents into one's ego.

Fear of Losing the Body or Physical Appearance

The fear of one's own death is one of the major fears in our culture. Since the ego places so much emphasis on the body rather than on the Divine Self that continues to exist after death, the loss of the body is a frightening thing. Some religions make their members worry about going to hell. When these people get close to life's end, their egos do not like the thought of possibly going to hell or of ending up being nothing but dust in a grave.

There are also fears associated with the loss of the ideal social images of how the body should look. The thoughts of becoming old and no longer looking like a young, beautiful woman or a handsome man are prevalent fears. This is especially true for those who have relied on their appearance as the main ego way for evaluating their self-worth. There are those who fear gaining weight, and some of them become anorexic and carry out extreme measures to lose it.

Fear of Loss of Power

Power and control over others, as opposed to love, are central values of the ego consciousness. Since the ego operates for the good-of-me, it wants to control circumstances and people to get what it wants. Have you noticed a person at work or in churches, social groups, and the family who has a strong attachment to being the boss or the one in control? Such people also have the fear of losing their power, and they strike out to defend it when necessary.

My wife's guilt and my complaining were ways of struggling for control in the family. Our egos reacted with strong emotions to try to defend what we thought was our piece of the financial power to control family money.

Power Conflicts Make for Unhappy Relationships

Terrorists know that if they can put fear into enemies, they can control them. Fear is a means of controlling others. Political parties use the fear of terrorism, communism, or socialism, or other fears such as someone taking your guns or losing Medicare, or losing other things to get votes and gain control.

When I was a fundamentalist Christian, the church used the fear of hell as a means of control. I eventually concluded that there was no hell to fear, since it seemed that humans were quite capable of all ego wickedness by themselves.

When I was in Eckankar™, the leaders told the members that if they left the religion, they would have serious karmic difficulties and would lose their initiations. After leaving Eckankar for five years, the organization sent a letter informing me that it was erasing my name and initiations from their database. It seemed they were trying to instill fear in me to rejoin or I would have to start over from the bottom. I thought that since initiations were only based on the time I spent in Eckankar™ and paying membership fees rather than on any visible spiritual progress I had made, then why should I worry about losing them?

In addition, the Eckankar™ fear of difficulties happening to me if I left never came true, so why should I be concerned about losing initiations? They had little to do with my current spirituality. I have had a blessed life, with a lot more spiritual growth since I left Eckankar™. Fear motivates people to act irrationally and to imprison their consciousness. We need to be aware of others who try to manipulate us with fears of excommunication, which place us in their ego prisons.

Has anyone ever tried to manipulate you with fear to do or not to do something?

> **Don't Let Military Boots of Fear and Control March Through Your Mind**

Fear of the Loss of Things

The ego loves things and forms strong attachments to them. When people lose things, it can get them so upset that they act irrationally. I was burglarized about 30 years ago in Kentucky, and I was upset about losing things I was attached to. I felt angry and uneasy about burglars violating my personal space and about the state police not doing anything about it, even though we knew who did it. Fortunately, I did not become irrational and follow through with the angry thought I had about burning down the burglar's house.

More recently, when our home was burglarized in Minnesota, my reaction was different. I was not attached to the objects that were stolen, since they were just things. I have to admit that I did have attachment to one thing, a necklace my father gave my wife. It was hand-cut from an old coin. Since my father was deceased, and he had created the necklace, I felt a sentimental attachment to it, but even this attachment passed away quickly.

These experiences told me that I was making some progress over ego's attachments. After the Minnesota burglar was caught, I learned that he burglarized houses in Oregon and had burned them down. I wondered how my previous thoughts in Kentucky, of wanting the burglar's house burned down, almost brought me dangerously close to receiving the karmic consequences of my own house being burned down.

Do you find yourself overly attached to something and do you emotionally react if its loss is threatened?

Ego Is Fear-based

Fear of the Future

Fear of my financial future is probably my strongest fear. Most of my complaining was motivated by this fear. Not knowing what is going to happen in my financial future still pushes my reaction buttons slightly, but not like it used to.

***

While using one of Brian L. Weiss's CDs to do a past life regression, I asked why I had such a fear of my financial future. In the experience, I was looking at my feet, and they were the feet of a black man. I was thin, and I wore a Caribbean shirt and shorts. It seemed that I was on the borderline of being poor, and I lived alone in a thatched house. I had a treasure box that had all of my earthly valuables in it, and I seemed to be taking an inventory of them and admiring my possessions.

In the next scene, I was in my house and robbers were trying to get me to tell where I hid my treasure box. I refused to tell them. The next thing I knew, they cut off my right leg at the knee with a machete, so I gave them what they wanted. The third scene showed me as a miserable, one-legged, homeless old man begging in the streets. I assumed that with only one leg, I couldn't do whatever work I had done before, and had to become a beggar.

Wow! If that wouldn't put the fear of the future in me, I don't know what would. It was an experience that instilled the fear of a negative financial future in my consciousness, and I'm still feeling the effects of it in this lifetime. Many fears are rooted in past lives.

***

Experiencing this past life helped me understand my fear at a deeper level, but it did not automatically dispel my fear of the future. When the financial fear arises now, I use this past life experience to help stop the fear from spreading like a wildfire. I tell it, "What happened in a past life doesn't mean it has to happen now. My future is going to be fine." Instead of letting the ego react, I trust the Divine to do what is best for all. This stops the energy of the fear from reaching my crown *chakra* at the top of the head, where it could block spirit from entering my body. This *chakra* serves as an open portal for the flow of divine love and wisdom.

Recognizing that my fear was caused by a past life experience was the deeper level of recognition. First, I recognized the habit of complaining, then I recognized my fear of future financial insecurity that caused my ego reactions, and finally, I recognized that the root cause of the fear was in a past life experience. The last level of recognition is helpful, but it is not absolutely necessary for changing ego habits and fears.

The ego loves to live in the past or future. Since I like to live in the future, it tends to increase the fear of uncertainty. I tend to view my financial future as negative, but I also view the future as an opportunity for change that can bring good into my life. This makes the present into a means to an end. Eventually, I learned, especially after reading Eckhart Tolle's book, *The Power of Now* that my focus should be on the present moment rather than on using it as a means for realizing a successful future. *The ego self is past-based and future-based.* Being spiritual and living with love is now-based.

The future and the past are where worrying originates. When I focused on the future, it almost always led to worrying in the present. Now that I know the Divine will take care of the future if I take care of the present moment, I worry less.

> ***Living in the Present is a No Worry Zone***

Do you fear the uncertainty of your future?

Fear of God

I took my mother, who was in her 90s to a grocery store, and I wanted to park as close to the door as possible in order to make it easier for her to walk. I was waiting for a car to pull out, and I saw a car next to where we were waiting that had the sign, "**FEAR GOD**," on its back window. I thought to myself, *What about the scripture that says the first commandment is to love God?* The next thing I knew, the woman, who was putting groceries into that car, came over and shoved a pamphlet through the window into Mom's hand. I thought that was kind of pushy and rude.

I can remember when I believed in the wrath of God and feared Him. When difficulties came into my life, I thought it was God bringing them. Most of the time, I could not connect the difficulties to any sin I had committed, and I wondered why God was punishing me. God's wrath was like the random force of luck that I never knew when or why I would have to experience. Random punishment was an effective way of putting the fear of God in me.

I'm glad I eventually realized that my relationship with God should not be based on fear. It should instead be love. I feel sorry for those who live their lives imprisoned in this religious dogma of the fear of God. There are enough ego fears already, and we do not need religions pilling more on top of what already exists. God is pure love and wants a relationship with us based on pure love.

I saw on an outdoor church sign a week before Easter that read, "We use duct tape to fix things. God uses nails." I could feel the pain of nails piercing my hands and feet, and it made me sick to my stomach. I thought, *That was an awful cruel thing to say, and besides, the Divine uses love to fix things.* If I didn't know better, that imagery of God pounding nails into my hands and feet would have made me fear God earlier in life when I was a Christian. Ego religions project their own negative beliefs on what they want God to be like. Pounding nails into your hands rather than the nonjudgmental and unconditional love that God gives to all.

If fear is the basis of your relationship with the Divine, I would suggest that you start looking for another religion or just be the most loving person you can be. *Where there is love, fear cannot exist.*

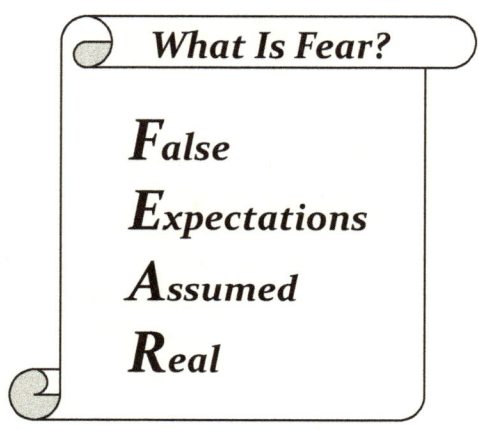

What Is Fear?

*F*alse
*E*xpectations
*A*ssumed
*R*eal

As I said, the list of fears was not a comprehensive list, but you might have recognized some of the ones listed happening in your own life. Recognizing them is important for controlling the ego consciousness since fear is one of the underlying motivations of behavior. Fears are behind our ego reactions and they are more difficult to recognize than the ego habits themselves.

Ego Reacts Unconsciously to Protect Itself

The problem with the ego consciousness is that those who are under its influence do not know it. They are literally in the dark. I was for a long time unaware of the power that the ego had over my life, and I learned even more about its scope of influence while writing this book. The ego operates in an unconscious reactive mode, since its beliefs, values, attitudes, fears, and experiences are stored in the subconscious mind, the part of the mind that automatically and unconsciously reacts to life's circumstances. *Ego self is unconscious-based and reactive-based.*

When this happens, the ego self is in full control. We are operating out of what cognitive neuroscientists refer to as the subconscious mind. This is the storehouse where the unconscious thoughts, beliefs, emotions, instincts, fears, and habits reside that determines most of our behavior.

According to cell biologist Bruce H. Lipton and Steve Bhaerman, in the book, *Spontaneous Evolution,* the subconscious mind controls approximately "95 percent of our decisions, actions, emotions, and behaviors." That's most of what we do. Since the subconscious mind operates by unconscious habits, compulsions, reactions, and drives, we are very much like programmed robots reacting to life's external circumstances. Consequently, we end up being slaves to the automatic responses of the ego's habits stored in the subconscious mind, which blocks our connection with the Divine.

In the book, *The Biology of Belief,* Lipton characterizes the subconscious mind as a powerful processor of information. It can process 20 million bits of stimuli per second from the external environment, while the conscious mind can only process 40 bits of stimuli per second. Is it any wonder that we are more like robots that automatically respond to external commands than are like highly conscious, self-directed persons? The powerful subconscious mind can easily take over your life with the ego habits stored there. This unconscious behavior works against being a conscious spiritual and loving person.

Fortunately, there is one way to overcome or eliminate the ego's unconscious power, by consciously storing spiritual habits or love in the subconscious mind. When we then react, it will be with love. Love will then be our primary motivation energizing life.

> **Filling a Subconscious Mind with Spiritual Habits Leaves No Room for Ego's Habits**

The purpose of the ego self is to assure the continual survival of its illusionary identity and ego realities. To accomplish this, it must do whatever is necessary to protect itself. My complaining assumed that others (my wife) were at fault, and that I was the victim. Consequently, my ego reacted by complaining in order to assert power over my wife and to protect my ego self by maintain the illusion that she caused our financial insecurity.

> **Ego Is Insecure and Struggles to Protect Itself**

My complaining judged my wife as the source of our financial problems, while protecting my ego's superior status. Counterattacks on my righteous ego seemed unfair, and being machine-gunned to death with bullets of guilt made me feel like a victim. The ego hates and fears whatever threatens its illusions. To protect itself, the ego reacts and tries to attack others through anger, complaining, gossip, guilt, vanity, and other ego responses.

There will be a natural tendency for you as a reader to react to some of the things I am saying about the ego, especially when it applies to you. If you find yourself reacting, take note of it, since the reaction might be one of those unconscious ego habits you will need to deal with at some point in your life.

How do you defend your ego self?

> ### LOG EYE
>
> ***I complain about splinters in others' eyes,***
> ***But am satisfied with petrified logs in my eye.***
>
> ***My ego protects my log,***
> ***Like it's a ferocious junkyard watchdog.***
>
> ***While only the Light of love can replace a log,***
> ***Like the rays of the sun dissipates fog.***

Since the ego is stored within the subconscious and unconsciously reacts with negative responses such as greed, fear, conflict, unhappiness, and dogma, these are the reasons why the ego needs to be recognized. In a later chapter, this recognition will be discussed as ego-realization.

We are living in the Ego Age, where we have arrived at an evolutionary place in history where the ego has become so powerful with its technology, dangerous, and dysfunctional that it may lead to our extinction. However, you have a choice that can change this dangerous trend.

One of the major choices in life is to determine what you want as your true identity. Will it be the ego self or Divine Self? Too many choose the ego, and this is why today's world is so unhappy, violent, polarized, and filled with negativity. There is a great need to topple the ego self from its throne of dominance and to replace it with the Divine Self. This is the topic of the next chapter.

Figure 3.1

SUGGESTED QUESTIONS FOR PERSONAL AND GROUP DISCUSSION
1. Have you had an experience where love set you free from your ego's habits?
2. Have you ever tried stopping an ego habit that damaged relationships with others?
3. What is your main attachment in life?
4. Do you fear abandonment?
5. Do you fear losing your social status or self-worth?
6. Do you fear losing your body or physical appearance?
7. Do you fear loss of power?
8. Do you fear the loss of some of your most prized material possessions?
9. Do you fear the uncertainty of the future?
10. What other types of fears do you have?
11. How do you control your fears?
12. Are you ego-realized?

☺ *Smile* ☺
The ego is only a temporary mental concept,
But your true self is an eternal being of light and love.

Chapter Four

Love Flows from the Divine Within

I wasn't a rebellious youth, but as a teenager, I sensed a hollow emptiness in my life as well as in the lives of my parents, as I mentioned earlier. I was probably uncomfortable with my ego identity as well as with my parents' lack of religion. I sensed something was missing, but I didn't know for sure what it was.

One Easter Sunday, when I was thirteen or fourteen, I decided to attend the local Methodist Church. I took my younger brother with me for moral support, since I didn't know what to expect.

This church experience led me to a different view of who I was. I learned I was born in sin and was a sinner. I felt my body was the devil incarnated. I was taught that sex was a sin, even when having a child. In contrast, Eckhart Tolle, a modern day spiritual teacher, believes sex is a spiritual desire for oneness with the Divine. In his book, *The Power of Now*, he said, "Sexual union is the closest you can get to this state [oneness] on the physical level. This is why it is the most deeply satisfying experience the physical realm can offer." This view is a galaxy apart from what I was taught as a Christian.

I was a sinner, and I had to believe in Jesus as the only begotten Son of God, who died for my sins. If I felt guilty enough and repented, my sins were forgiven and I was saved to go to heaven.

Later in life, I learned that this belief about being a sinner in need of salvation was not something Jesus taught. It was added as a doctrine to try to make sense of Jesus's crucifixion. The church also used it to gain control of its members by making them feel guilt about their sin of killing Jesus. This was an example of how the ego consciousness of church leaders used fear and guilt to control church members.

Religious Beliefs Can Negatively Affect Your Self Image

Soul was another aspect of my identity that Christianity taught, but it was confusing to me as a teenager. The church said I had a soul, something like an invisible spirit that hangs around waiting for me to die. I also learned I would be this soul for the rest of eternity. While living on earth, I was the ego self with a spiritual appendage hanging around that I would slip into after death. I therefore believed I was a body that had a soul, rather than being Soul that had a body. Soul was consequently of no importance as a source of identity while I was living. But at least I was introduced to the belief that there was another part of me that would be spirit someday.

The church's belief about the end of time, where my physical body would rise from the grave in its physical form to be with Jesus, was an additional confusion. I wondered. Would I be my body or soul at the end of time? Since the church was attached to the physical form of the body and to its ego identity, I thought I might have a physical body even in the afterlife.

Love Flows from the Divine Within

***

Years later, when I worked as a Job Corps teacher in North Carolina, I had a supervising principal who belonged to the Lions Club. He asked me and others to donate our eyes when we died. When I signed my donation form, he told me about a man who had refused to sign.

The man had said to him, "I need my eyes when I rise from the grave at the end of time to be with Christ."

That's what I probably would have believed earlier in my life, and I might have refused to donate my eyes too. Even though I was confused about whether I would ultimately be spirit or human flesh in the spiritual worlds, I still identified myself with my earthly body, ego mind, and emotions. My Christian beliefs about being soul after death didn't do much to change my identity, but it did confuse me. As a Methodist and then as a Quaker, I viewed myself primarily as the ego self.

***

I wish I'd had the Internet when I was younger, since I could have read about Henry's innovative way of getting into heaven. He had found a loophole to allow him enter heaven with his ego fully intact. Henry's mother was exasperated with his mischievous behavior and asked him, "How do you expect to get into heaven, Henry?"

Henry thought for a while and said, "Well, I'll run in and out, and in and out, and keep slamming the door until St. Peter says, 'For heaven's sake, Henry, come in or stay out!'"

***

Another church belief I had about the human body was that it had the same image as God. Consequently, I thought God was an old white man with a beard. Not only would soul look like my body, but God looked human too. I didn't realize, at the time, that my church was attached to the outer form or image of the body, believing that it would not only exist in the physical world but would exist in the afterlife as well.

***

This was probably why Archie Bunker and George Jefferson of the *All in the Family* TV program, one of my favorite old-time shows, differed in their opinions about how God looked. In one of the episodes, Archie Bunker told George, "Every one of the pictures I've seen, God is white."

George Jefferson quickly retorted, "Maybe you're looking at the pictures' negatives."

Soul and Psychology

The next time I questioned my identity was as a student at West Virginia Wesleyan College. In my psychology class, the professor gave a lecture about personal identity. He talked about the body, mind, emotions, and personality and about some social aspects that identified the self. For some reason, I reacted to what he was saying and asked him after class, "Where does soul fit into the picture?"

Since this was a class in a Methodist college, I thought soul should have something to do with my identity. But his response was, "In psychology, we do not deal with soul. It's outside the parameters of scientific investigation."

He didn't dare acknowledge that we became soul after death, as the church taught. Even in a religious college, science can ignore soul by defining it out of the realm of investigation. I didn't realize then that I was carrying around some kind of inner awareness that who I was had something to do with being Soul. It wasn't until much later in life that the issue of my true identity surfaced.

Love Flows from the Divine Within

Most psychological and social sciences are dogmatic about the existence of the ego identity while ignoring the Soul, our true identity. Most university scientists, regardless of their ego beliefs about having open minds, operate like they belong to a faith-based church and refuse to consider the possibility of a Divine Self. Fortunately, there are some transpersonal psychologists and sociologists and a few others in academic institutions who consider humans as spiritual beings. There is at least a small light of understanding shining in our higher academic institutions.

Ego Transformation

In the early 1970s, while I was in Eckankar™, I learned I didn't *have* a soul, but I *am* Soul right now. I didn't have to wait until after death to become Soul. I was already Soul, a divine being.

I also learned that Soul was an eternal spark of God. Therefore, I was a being with divine qualities, and Soul was my primary and everlasting identity. Soul existed from one incarnation to another, but it took on different body shells that allowed me to operate in the world of matter. This was possibly what I had known intuitively earlier in my life, which had stirred my search for religion and had caused me to question my psychology professor. Initially, I only had a mental concept of myself being Soul. It took years of spiritual experiences to learn more about myself as Soul. I'm still trying to fully realize and practice that *I am Soul*.

Once I realized I was Soul, my beliefs changed. I now believed that Soul, and not the body, was what the Bible meant when it said we were "made in the image of God." Soul is spirit or pure energy, and this, rather than a physical looking body, is the image of God.

I was also taught earlier by Christianity that the body was the "temple of the living God," but I did not understand what the "living God" meant. I now know that Soul is the "living God" that lives within the body's temple. This body/temple houses the "living God." When I view the body as a temple, it is no longer a sinful thing. The Bible and church doctrine have contradictory beliefs about who I am, and I prefer to believe I'm in the image of the "living God."

Since I have to take care of my physical house to have a healthy body, I also learned that I had to take care of my body as the home of Soul. Soul needs a clean house or temple, with no ego distractions, in order to be a focused, joyful resident living in the presence of the Divine.

The body's value is in giving Soul a temporary, earthly temple where it can help function as the Divine's legs and arms to create and for distributing love in a material world. I have even come to believe that the body's cells also have their share of divine awareness, and that they also serve as our spiritual partners in the co-creative process.

An unhealthy body makes Soul's work more difficult. That is why the body sends warning signals of pain when we are not taking care of it. Pain is a throbbing warning sign, telling us to learn, change, or heal something in order to allow pure energy to balance the body back to health.

Over time, I gradually replaced my negative ego identity and came to know myself as a Divine Self. I am a divine energy spark from the Divine Source, a part of the whole. I will never be the Divine Source, but I may become divine-like. It took me a while, but I now know that I am Soul. Being a divine being, I now have the power of creation, where I'm responsible for choosing my own destiny and that of the world.

> *I'm Soul a Creative Power House of Love*

Experiencing the Golden Energy Soul

Sometime during the latter part of the 1970s, I attended a seminar where there were several thousand in attendance. About fifteen or twenty minutes into the session, I looked out over the crowd from the back of the auditorium. I felt uplifted. The collective consciousness of the group helped produce heightened vibrations within me. My focus on physical objects turned blurry, and I saw dark outlines of images of people sitting or walking. A golden hue filled the auditorium. I had experienced the golden hue before, at other group meetings and when alone, but this time, something different happened.

I began to see bright, sparkling, golden globes of light that were a little smaller than the size of volleyballs, situated close to the back of the heads of a few people. This brilliant golden light emanating from them reminded me of a dynamo of creative liquid energy, and I could feel its peace and love. It emanated the most brilliant golden color I had ever seen.

The other people were like dark shadows, without any sign of these golden spheres. I wondered, *Why did a few have a golden light, while others didn't?* I noticed that some of these dark shadow people were walking toward the front of the auditorium to find seats, even though the session had already started. Maybe they were thinking like the ego does about being me-deep into themselves and didn't mind disturbing others to get a seat up front.

When I returned to everyday consciousness, I asked myself, *What did I just see*? I thought about possible explanations of what those brilliant spheres of golden light and energy might be.

I had seen the soft golden hue encompassing the auditorium at previous times, but not the bright, golden spheres behind people's heads. I believed the golden hue was the inner Light of the Soul dimension. However, these brilliant spheres of golden light that I saw didn't seem to be an inner plane or dimension.

Was I seeing a golden halo like the ones surrounding the heads of Jesus and other saints in paintings and pictures? If so, they didn't encircle the heads like any halo I had seen in paintings. They were more like imperfectly shaped spheres situated behind and toward the top of the head.

After the session, I told my wife about this experience, but she didn't know what those spheres were either. Since they were golden, I suspected that they might have something to do with the soul body, but that was only a guess. The bodies with the dark shadows might have been the ones whose ego imprisoned their golden Divine Self inside the body. Since I wasn't sure what I saw, I didn't tell others about my experience, for fear they might think I went a little off the deep side. Since my wife already knew that, telling her didn't matter.

***

When I attended West Virginia Wesleyan College as a student, there was mandatory chapel attendance every week. During my last two years, I refused to attend most of the chapels, even though I would lose some of my course credits. The ego resentment against forced chapel attendance carried over to Westminster College, where I was a faculty member. Even though attendance wasn't required at chapel, I did not attend a chapel service during the six years I taught there until the last week, just before leaving

I sat behind the chaplain of the college, and since the pews were close, his head was probably a foot or so from my face. At one point during the service, the chapel was filled with a golden hue, and when I looked at the head of the chaplain seated in front of me, he had the brightest golden sphere I had ever seen. The brightness might have occurred because I sat so close to him, or maybe it was because he had an exceptionally bright soul body. I didn't expect a member of the Christian clergy, who was mainly involved in outward rituals and dogmatic beliefs, to have such a shining golden Soul body. This experience jolted me into learning a lesson about judging the spirituality of a group of people. Spiritual growth is a personal experience and is not limited to or excluded from any religious or nonreligious Soul.

***

Soul Body Can Be Seen as Golden Light

Many of my spiritual experiences or observations were not usually completely understood at the time I experienced them, and I had to go through a period where I had to interpret them. After having experiences of the golden soul for several years, at other group meetings and at home, I reached a more satisfying interpretation. I concluded that I was seeing the Divine Self or what some refer to as the soul body. It was the manifestation of Soul as golden light or energy, but it was only the form image and was not the full aspect of what Soul is.

I had heard that Plato saw Soul as a golden entity, either residing near the head of a person or following him or her from a distance. Plato also said Soul could be entrapped inside the body. Maybe those with an entrapped Soul were the people I saw as dark shadows.

***

How many enlightened Souls does it take to screw in a light bulb? None. Since they can see by their own Inner Light, they do not need external lights. But enlightened people do what is good-for-All and are happy to install a light bulb to help others see.

***

I don't want to give the impression that the golden soul body is all that Soul is. Soul is a divine being and is therefore omnipresent. It is not confined to our heads, but consciousness can be anywhere it focuses its attention. It is all-present in the physical and spiritual worlds. The focusing of conscious attention determines where and what Soul experiences.

I'm not just my physical body, achievements, accumulation of material things, social and career status, mental capabilities, and other such ego-based things. More importantly, I'm also a divine being, and so is everyone else. I've also felt the golden, Divine Self as love, and I know I'm love too.

Since you, too, are of the likeness of the Divine, love yourself as the Divine Self rather than the ego. If you want to love the Divine, then love yourself as Soul. If you are searching for the Divine, the search will end with the spiritual image of your own Soul. I would also like to add that our divine likeness or essence appears as brilliant, golden atoms of the divine's manifested energy of love. As Soul, I'm already love. To be the true me is to be love.

I'm Love

Have you ever had an experience where you felt you were more than your physical or ego body?

A major paradigm shift in consciousness from the ego self to the Divine Self is starting. This will create changes in individual lives, which will be followed by changes in the collective consciousness of the world. This outcome, however, depends on whether people like you choose to know and be Soul.

Do you believe you are the Divine Self???

Most humans are the only creatures refusing to recognize who they are. What matters is not success in the social world, but realizing your true self as Soul. If you are wondering, what is my purpose in life? One of them while being here on earth is to recognize your true self as the Divine Self.

> **Soul, the Golden Sparkling Atom of the Divine**
>
> *I once thought I was a sinful, worldly ego self,*
>   *Imprisoned in a physical body of matter.*
>
> *When I saw the vibrant, golden sparkling self,*
>   *I knew I was more than the ego and mind's clatter.*
>
> *I'm divine golden energy atoms and one with the whole,*
>   *And thankful I'm a free, golden, sparkling Soul.*

Do you believe your true self is the ego self? If so, do as little Mary did and repeat the affirmation, "I'm sole." Or better yet, say, "I'm Soul." Just know and feel that the answer to the question—*Who am I?*—is Soul, a golden spark of Divine Energy.

> **We're Created with the Divine's Happy Face,**
> **But Prefer the Ego's Mean False Face**

The next two chapters will discuss the second shift. It is a shift from the ego consciousness of being a polarized body separate from others to being unified with them and with the Divine in a state of oneness. In these two chapters, you will discover that you are an energy being with powerful energy tools of love.

Figure 4.2

> **SUGGESTED QUESTIONS FOR PERSONAL AND GROUP DISCUSSION**
> 1. What is your answer to the question, "Who am I?"
> 2. Did your perception of who your true self was change during your lifetime? If so, how?
> 3. Do you now view your true self as Soul or the Divine Self?
> 4. Have you ever experienced the golden energy body of Soul?
> 5. What is the basic motivation in your life?
> 6. How do you create the things you want in your life?
> 7. Have you experienced Soul being the conscious observer of your ego habits?
> 8. Have you ever used Soul's power just to be something you wanted to be?
> 9. Have you ever experienced being one with the Divine?

☺ *Smile* ☺
You're a divine golden energy being.
Have you discarded your ego's false face and rags?

SHIFT II

Ego Polarization to Spiritual Oneness

The ego self views its identity as a physical, mental, and social entity that is separate from other humans and animals, or from plant life, the earth's environment, and the Divine. Separation creates polarization and the desire to dominate, which is evident in today's political parties and in dissension throughout the world. Humans at their quantum level are energy beings and are made of the same energy that is in all life and all earthly materials. When we view life from the perspective of being quantum energy fields, it becomes possible to realize spiritual oneness, and this becomes the basis for unity and for living in peace with all life and environments. We are energy beings or fields connected to ever-broadening energy fields, which unites us at the quantum level, as opposed to what occurs when our egos view themselves as separate. A shift away from ego polarization and toward oneness and harmony is necessary for creating with love.

Chapter Five

You're an Energy Being United with Others

Albert Einstein revolutionized the understanding of energy with his formula **$E=mc^2$**. The formula tells us that "energy" (E) equals "mass" (m) times the speed of light squared (c^2). In essence, despite the solid appearance of all material forms such as tables, houses, bodies, and so on, they are all energy atoms at their quantum levels, held together by universal forces. In the last four chapters, we discussed the body, the ego, and the Divine Self, which are nothing more than energy fields. You, therefore, are in essence an energy being.

When my family helped edit this chapter, my wife read this section just before she had cataract surgery. Not being a scientist, she read the formula **$E=mc^2$** as "E = me too." We all laughed, but this was a spiritual truth channeled through her to remind us that we were all energy too.

The formula also informs us that energy can be transformed into mass, or material things, and that material things can be transformed back into energy. At the city of Hiroshima, in Japan, an ounce of material plutonium became an atomic energy bomb, which caused great destruction.

Universe is Nothing More Than Energy, Including Me Too

Human Beings Are Energy Beings

Everything in the universe derives from unmanifested energy, which is derived from the Divine Source. The Divine Energy and Divine Self are also realms where unmanifested or formless energy exists. At these levels, we are in a state of oneness and unity with all. Before birth, as spirit, we lived in unity, but when we entered the world of duality where the ego exists, we shifted into a state of duality, separateness, and polarization. This is why a spiritual being eventually remembers and strives to return to its original state of oneness and unity with all.

As the unmanifested energy emerges from its source of love, it transforms into different manifested forms of matter in the worlds of duality. These forms include the dimensions of the subtle energy fields, the physical body, the mental and emotional fields, and all other physical matter. Even matter is derived from the unmanifested energy of the Divine Source, which means that it is in a state of unity and oneness with all other matter. We are therefore derived from one common energy source, and we have oneness with all types of matter as well as with spirit.

When this oneness with all is realized, we know we are in a state of unity with all. It is mental ego energy that believes itself to be separate from others as well as from its physical and spiritual environments.

Being an energy being in a state of oneness with all is one of the little known aspects of who we are. The ego focuses on the physical body, and the spiritual energy and Divine Self go unnoticed. The biological, social, and psychological sciences primarily focus attention on the body and its unconscious mental, emotional, and social aspects without realizing it as a source of energy with transformative spiritual powers. It is time to shift our consciousness toward the realization of the unity experienced by the Divine Self and away from the ego's desires for separateness, conflict, and polarization.

Interconnected Energy Fields

Fortunately, quantum physics, evolutionary biology, and other research have begun opening up the hidden identity of who we are as energy beings. During the last century, quantum physics questioned the basic premises of Newton's classical physics with its focus on physical matter as separate from other forms of matter.

At the subatomic level, electrons circle neutrons and protons at high speeds and at great distances from each other. When nuclear and electromagnetic forces bind these energy entities together, they form atoms. Atoms are at the root of what makes a body, which is a dynamo of energy or of quantum energy fields. These energy atoms are 90–99.9 percent empty space, but they appear as solid matter when they become entangled with each other. In reality, they are only energy fields containing a lot of empty space.

I'm not sure if it's true, since I have not experienced it, nor has science verified it, but the *Kryon* books by Lee Carroll believe that this empty space is the storage place for the love force in the universe. If this is true, then every atom is a storehouse of love energy, which makes the power of love plentiful and vastly available.

The body has trillions of cells, but I have not seen any estimate of the number of atoms in a human body. The number would be mind-boggling. To build the human body, atoms are entangled, and they cooperate and combine to form cells, organs, and body systems (e.g., nervous, vascular, and digestive), which are interrelated energy fields of various sizes. It was interesting when I learned that x-rays and MRIs do not take pictures of bones or organs, but rather take pictures of the energy fields of these body parts.

In the book, *Earth Dance,* evolutionary biologist Elisabet Sahtouris explains how we are living in an interconnected layer of fields that are ever increasing in size, from the smallest form of life to the size of the Earth and of the universe itself. Life is a dance of these connected partners of fields, which affect each other and which usually live in harmony rather than dominate and exploit each other. If we continue the ego way of domination, we will receive the consequences of our unwise actions, which harm these balanced interconnections in nature and in all life. Realizing how we are united is the way of love.

Fields in the body and those that surround the body as subtle energy bodies are interrelated with other fields. We are interconnected in an ever-widening expansion of energy fields. We are not separate entities, but are connected with other energy fields, which makes it possible for us to affect each other either adversely or beneficially. Energy systems unite in greater fields of interconnection, starting at the micro level and moving up to the physical body, to the universe, and ultimately connecting to the Divine Source itself. The idea that the ego is a separate entity is simply not true. We and the rest of the world are broadening circles of interconnected energy fields or systems.

The amazing thing is how all of these energy fields are coordinated in order to create and to maintain a balanced state of life. The body works in harmony without any conscious efforts to make it happen. This way of functioning is the model of cooperation and peace that humans should adopt in their social relationships, learning to be in balance and in harmony with all other energy fields.

***

One day, when I watched the Dr. Oz show on TV, the doctor talked about how to lose belly fat. I was very interested in this, since I have a stomach that blows up like a balloon with

You're an Energy Being United with Others

lightning speed, whereas it is a very difficult and a slow process to flatten it.

I had success one time in reducing my belly fat, but as I get older, I can't find an easy way to do it. According to microbiologist Bruce H. Lipton in *The Biology of Belief*, thoughts can affect DNA. When I heard this, I decided to talk to the fat DNA cells in my belly and tell them that they were no longer needed. I told them, "I no longer live in the age of hunting and gathering when belly fat was needed for periods of food shortages, and I want you to dissolve yourself and pass out of my body." Unfortunately, I have found that my belly fat cells were either really dumb, couldn't understand English, or were rebellious teenager cells refusing to listen. They didn't want to go away.

At times, I talk aloud to them when I'm alone and when no one is around. As I'm writing this, I'm hoping there are no psychiatrists reading this book, since I'm not sure if talking to fat cells is a sign of having a more serious mental problem than talking to God. I just want to let the psychiatrists know that I have never heard my fat cells talk back to me, so please do not send a paddy wagon to get me.

As for the rest of the Dr. Oz's belly fat story, one of the devices he demonstrated was a laser that burst fat cells, which then eventually passed out of the body. The woman who demonstrated the machine said it took a few sessions with the laser to dissolve some of the fat cells, and then the fat cells started communicating with each other to instruct the other fat cells to dissolve on their own. I thought this was a neat example of how cells were interrelated and were able to communicate and cooperate with each other. I wish my belly fat cells would start listening and would pass the exodus information to my other fat cells, since I can't afford the $3,000 or more for the laser work.

***

Chapter 1 included an illustration of the subtle body energy fields that surround the physical body. These fields mediate energy and information between Soul and the body. Because these added layers of energy fields vibrate higher than physical energy fields, the human eye cannot see them. They include the etheric or intuitive fields, the emotional fields, the memory fields, and mind energy fields that are referred to by some as the human aura. In addition, there is the Divine Self energy field, which should be in charge of all the other subtle human energy fields.

People with high-level energy vibrations can see these energy fields as light and can hear them as sound. Subtle body fields provide the life force energy, which does much of the coordinating of the zillions of things needed to maintain life.

Additionally, there are collective energy fields of social groups. The Earth itself has an energy field, which is known as the earth's magnetic field. All of these fields interact with each other and can affect each other, according to Elisabet Sahtouris.

You as an energy being extend your energy influence much farther out than the boundary of your outer skin. This is why it is important for you to be the best person of love and peace that you can be. Since your energy fields also affect the energy fields of family, coworkers, and friends as well as the community, the nation, and even the world, what you think, feel, imagine, and do is important. If you change to be more loving, the world is also affected. Whatever you are within, the world will be without. This is why you can change the world by simply changing yourself.

So Within, So Without

The energy fields that exist inside and outside of you provide the life force that creates and maintains life, provides a doorway to direct divine experiences, holds the key to co-create with divine thoughts, is the home of your Divine Self, connects us to each other, and changes the world. You energy fields are of utmost importance for world peace, joy, and freedom when you are living a realization of the connectivity of love.

Experiencing Energy Fields

For most of my life, I was ignorant of energy fields. I had some experiences later that helped me understand some things such as the golden energy field of the Divine Self. It wasn't until I wrote this book that I began to understand energy fields fuller importance for my spiritual life and for the Love Age.

I believe the first time I heard about auras was when Audrey introduced me to Edgar Cayce's books. Cayce could see the colored lights produced by energy fields emanating around the bodies of people. He used these auras to pinpoint health problems and was able to suggest remedies for restoring health. I can remember wishing I could experience seeing auras.

Eventually, I was able to see them. I never had much control over this type of experience, but when I squinted my eyes or received a boost of energy from a group's higher vibration level, it helped. The experience was usually spontaneous. I can't remember the first time I saw an aura, but there are a few I'd like to share.

***

In the mid-1990s, I worked for the State of California. One day, my boss was sitting in a chair conducting a departmental meeting. I sat on the other side of the table, listening to her. My eyes started to go out of focus and a green colored light surrounded the top part of her body, since that was the only part I could see above the level of the table. This phenomenon lasted for about a minute and disappeared as my eyes returned to a clear focus of the room. I saw this aura several other times at meetings.

I wondered why I only saw a green aura as the predominate color surrounding her. I recalled from Edgar Cayce's books that green related to people who pursued medical professions, but she wasn't in that field. However, in Shabda Yoga the color green related to the earth plane consciousness, and she was very much oriented toward ego worldly success.

Another experience happened about a decade or so ago, when I was at a worship service in Sacramento. A person that I respected for her spirituality and her loving nature was speaking about a personal experience. As she talked, I saw a golden aura surrounding her whole body. It was not like the sphere of golden light at the back of the head that I mentioned previously. The predominant color was golden on the outer ring, but there were other colors on the inner rings that were faint, which made them difficult to discern. Gold light, for me, represented Soul, the Divine Self. I could understand why I saw a golden aura around this loving Soul.

Auras Are Energy Fields

Have you ever seen an aura?

***

One of the strangest auras I ever saw was the aura of a tall pine tree. I had moved to a new home in the Sierra Mountains, surrounded by tall cedars and white pine trees. My son and I packed and unpacked the truck in the same day. If the neighbors had seen me slowly climb the two flights of stairs at the end of the move, they might have wondered if I was a 120 year-old man ready to keel over. I was at the point of total exhaustion.

I wondered, *was this move worth the effort? On Monday, I have to start an hour commute to work. Did Audrey and I make a mistake moving here?*

You're an Energy Being United with Others

Being among tall pine trees had always given me a sense of inner peace, and this was one of the main reasons for moving there. Even though I was exhausted, I decided to view the tall trees from the back patio before dusk turned to nighttime. When I leaned my aching body on the patio banister, my eyes began to blur. I wondered if I was going to faint. One pine tree stood out from the others, and I could see a light bluish and green colored light surrounding its outline. The light looked similar to the bluish/green flames of a gas-burning fireplace.

I blinked my eyes, thinking that there must be something in them, but the flaming colors were still there. I then received a telepathic thought, "All will be fine." I wondered what this meant. My eyes came back into focus, and I moved over to one of the patio chairs to rest my weary bones.

I had heard about long-distance runners getting so exhausted that they entered altered states of consciousness. My oldest son, Rob, had had this kind of experience while running track in high school. Was this what had happened to me when I saw the tree's aura? I had seen auras around people before, but I had never seen an aura around plant life. Was it the tree's aura? Then I turned my attention to the message, "All will be fine." Did that mean that the move was the right thing to do, even though the commute to work would be a longer one? I sure hoped so.

Later, I came to the conclusion that the tree channeled a divine message to comfort me. It also made me aware that the Divine could use anything to give messages of guidance, help, and comfort.

After about a year had passed, I watched a television movie about Moses, in which he saw a burning bush and received a message from it. The scene brought back the memory of the tree aura. It also brought back a childhood memory of being in a Sunday school class and seeing in a study guide a picture of Moses standing by a bush that was engulfed in flames. At that time, I thought it was impossible for a bush to burn, to continue to live, and to talk to Moses. I didn't believe this story at all.

When I remembered my own aura experience of the pine tree looking like it was outlined in a bluish/green flame, I wondered. Did Moses see a flame-like aura around the bush, as I had seen around the tree? That seemed to be a better explanation than the explanation of a bush on fire.

***

We are not the only things in the world that have auras or surrounding energy fields. Since everything is energy, everything has an aura that can be used to interrelate with other fields, and the Divine can use these auras to communicate with us.

Followers of Hinduism, Buddhism, and the Jewish Kabbalah as well as Christian, Mayan, Cherokee, and Incan mystics or other spiritual groups have reported seeing auras or light surrounding the body. These energy fields have been recognized for thousands of years or even longer by shamanistic practitioners. These fields were an integral part of their lives and their healing practices. It is only recently that scientists have begun to research energy bodies, and Western health practices are also starting to use Eastern energy healing.

My wife is a registered nurse and works at a university medical hospital that offered a course for nurses in *Reiki* energy healing. She took the course and found a new outlet for her compassion for helping others. Some of the nurses in the pediatric ward used this form of healing to help children. I'm not suggesting that the medical center has completely integrated *Reiki* healing into the hospital's medical practices. They are taking steps toward recognizing the importance of energy as a source of healing, beyond its use in taking x-rays and performing MRIs. In time, I expect it will be even more fully integrated into the health systems, as it is already used at other hospitals and clinics. Energy not only enlivens the body, but it also heals it.

Energy Field Research

Researchers are more aware of physical energy inside the body than of the energy fields surrounding it. Their ability to measure physical energy makes this possible. Every cell in the body is made of atoms and is like a rechargeable battery that creates and stores electrical and magnetic energy. Each atom in a cell operates like a charger, pulling energy from the universal source of energy. The biological cells then store this electric, magnetic field energy, and photons for their operations and maintenance. Energy fields exist not only around cells but also around the organs and even around the whole body.

Auras and Science

When I first saw auras around people, I wasn't aware that I was viewing energy fields or subtle energy bodies. I just thought of it as the light of God shining around us. Now researchers have begun to put together evidence of energy outside the body.

Energy fields surrounding the body are difficult to measure, but researchers have viewed some of their effects and have detected the transformation of subtle energy into physical energy in our bodies. Physicists refer to this field of energy surrounding and in our bodies as the Zero Point Field (ZPF). It not only exists inside and outside our bodies, but in the whole universe.

> ***Energy Is Abundant and Omnipresent***

Cyndi Dale, in her book, *The Subtle Body,* reports that science has used the Superconducting Quantum Interference Device (SQUID) to detect electromagnetic energy beyond the body. In other research, biophysics researcher Fritz-Albert Popp and other scientists found that there was a level of energy operating behind DNA's chemical processes. At this level, the DNA stored photons, units of light that emit electromagnetic energy and drive the body's processes. Popp and his associates also report that DNA responds to a field of light that surrounds the body.

Popp discovered that all life has a shining current of light emanating from it. For example, experiments with cancer patients found that their lights were dull and almost going out, but when the researchers observed healthy patients, those patients' biophotons vibrated at a "super powerful frequency" and shined brightly.

The University of California, Davis Center for Biophotonics Science and Technology recently used the power of light energy to image how HIV transmits itself. The transmission was different from what had been theorized, and the scientists now hope this new discovery will direct medical researchers toward new cures for HIV. The researchers are also working on cancer, trying to understand how it operates. It is heartening that energy research like this is expanding our ability to be better healers.

Physical & Spiritual Bodies are Energy & Emanate Light

Energy fields are sources of light that surround us and which contain information, emotions, thoughts, "life force" energy, memories, and spiritual love, among other types of energy. Many refer to these external sources of energy as subtle bodies or as spiritual energy. Since science has difficulty measuring this external energy directly, the energy's effects have to serve as indirect indicators of it.

Cyndi Dale reports that Dr. William Tiller, a research physicist at Stanford University, has detected these subtle energy fields surrounding the body. When these subtle energies convert to physical energy, Tiller was able to use a transducer signal at a magnetic vector to detect it. So far, using physical instruments to detect this transformation of energy is one way of inferring that they are detecting energy fields external to our body. In addition, these magnetic and electrical signals correlate with observable physical effects. Science is only beginning to study the energy aspects of humans, and I hope it expands its research in this area rather than continuing only to focus on the body's physical and chemical processes.

> *Science Ignoring Spiritual Energy Is Like*
> *Light Bulbs Trying to Shining without Electricity*

Spiritual people know they are energy beings connected to all other energy fields, and that this connection can help create harmony in the world. The ego believes it's alone in the world and needs to defend itself, which creates conflict and polarization. One of the highest spiritual experiences is to realize the oneness with all, which arises out of this interconnectedness of all energy fields. The next chapter continues the scientific validation of the concept of energy fields and examines how they work to create unity and harmony within and between the biological, environmental, social, and spiritual worlds.

Figure 5.1

> **SUGGESTED QUESTIONS FOR PERSONAL AND GROUP DISCUSSION**
> 1. Are you aware that you are a being of energy?
> 2. Have you ever seen an aura around another person?
> 3. Have you ever tried to go within to feel the energy field that surrounds your body?
> 4. Have you ever had an energy healing?
> 5. Have you ever experienced an aura around a plant or animal?

☺ *Smile* ☺
You're a powerful being of energy.
Are you using your energy to expand love in the world?

Chapter Six

Energy Fields and Spiritual Oneness

The spiritually enlightened have known that all of us derive from and connect to the unmanifested energy of the Divine Source. We are all made of the same substance. This is at the root of what spiritual masters have sought to experience as the oneness with all. This spiritual experience truly provides an inner source of peace and harmony with all others, with the environment, universe, and with the Divine.

If you have this spiritual goal, this is what you will eventually experience too. Enlightened beings' spiritual experiences of light, sound, and spiritual dimensions have helped to validate what scientists are beginning to find. For example, the mathematics of string theory, a more recent development of quantum physics, theorizes that six to eleven dimensions exist beyond our physical world. Most seem to think there are nine dimensions. These dimensions are no more than broad energy fields existing at different levels of vibrations.

I watched a NOVA documentary about string theory and one of the scientist theorized that there was only one dimension. I thought that was interesting since spiritual masters have been experiencing the universe, including the Divine, as one. At a higher level of consciousness, it is all experienced as one. But this does not exclude that there are other dimensions at other states of consciousness.

These levels, planes, or dimensions known by spiritual practitioners have varied from each other in number, description, and purpose. Since they are subtle energy fields with vague and difficult borders to discern, it is difficult to reach a consensus on their number.

Energy Fields are Also Spiritual Dimensions

The following list of spiritual dimensions is a starting point for our discussion of the energy levels existing beyond the body. I mentioned these briefly in the chapters about the Divine Self and the ego self, and to a degree illustrated them in Figure 1.1. I will list these levels again and will add a few alternative names in brackets.

- Divine Source [Loving Source, God, Divine]
- Divine Energy [Spirit, Holy Ghost, *Reiki*, Chi]
- Divine Self [Spiritual Mind, Soul]
- Mental subtle body [intellectual mind, analytical mind]
- Memory subtle body [causal, instinctive mind, subconscious mind]
- Emotional subtle body [astral, emotions]
- Intuitive subtle body [etheric]
- Physical body [Humans]

Spiritual seekers have experienced these energy levels or spiritual dimensions, and modern science is beginning to discover more about them. Today, more and more people are experiencing and realizing that we are more than the world of

Energy Fields and Spiritual Oneness

matter we detect with our senses. These energy fields are elements of our self, and we need to realize them in order to understand the energy power of love. This need is especially true, since this realization provides a doorway into the spiritual worlds, provides a source of spiritual wisdom and love, provides the power to change and heal ourselves, and is the essence that unifies us. Love is the most powerful energy in the universe, and these inner spiritual sources of energy are the source of divine love.

> ### *Love the Divine Self*
>
> ***Loving the body self,***
> ***Depends on others' approval & its loss is your pain.***
>
> ***Loving the ego self,***
> ***Creates vanity and others' disdain.***
>
> ***Loving the Divine Self,***
> ***Fills your tank with love's high octane.***

Transforming Subtle Energy into Physical Energy

Most believe we receive energy only from the food we eat and from the oxygen we breathe, but we also receive it from our subtle body's energy fields. How are subtle energy and its information surrounding our body transformed into physical energy and wisdom? Cyndi Dale describes the interface between the subtle energy fields and the body as channels or meridians throughout the body. These "rivers of light" pulsate with vital energy and transport energy into and around the person's body.

The body has organs that convert the subtle energy with its high vibrations into lower vibrating energy, so it's in a usable form for the body. Earlier in the book, these organs were compared to the transformers that reduce electrical power to homes in order to lower the power of electricity for use in appliances and in the computer I'm using to write this book.

Chakras Are the Transformers of Spiritual Energy

Eastern religions refer to these areas where subtle energy enters the body as *chakras*. W. A. Tiller, W. E. Dibble, Jr., and J. G. Kohane ("Conscious Acts of Creation: The Emergence of a New Physics," Pavior Publishing, 2001) experimented and found that the meridian and *chakra* areas of the body had higher electromagnetic energy when compared to other areas. This result suggests that these areas are the places where subtle energy transforms into lower vibrating physical energy. Consequently, *chakras* are the body's transformers as well as being portals into spiritual dimensions.

When people speak of body *chakras*, the number listed varies in range from four to twelve, but most people use a list of seven. Most Eastern religions also agree that when one progresses in consciousness from the first *chakra* to the seventh at the top of the head, the possibility of experiencing the Divine increases.

In case you are unfamiliar with *chakras*, the seven most commonly recognized *chakras* are as described in Figure 6.1. They are related to the organs and to the primary spiritual functions that are often associated with these incoming and outgoing energy centers.

If you are using these *chakras* for direct spiritual experiences in meditation, I would suggest using the sixth and seventh or feeling the collective essence of all of the subtle energy bodies. It is here that you can have the easiest and most direct experiences with the Divine. Not only does energy pour into us at the *chakra* areas, but they are also the doorways into the subtle energy fields, where you can experience inner spiritual dimensions.

Energy Fields and Spiritual Oneness

Figure 6.1

***Chakra* Centers and Spiritual Energy Functions**

CHAKRAS	BODY LOCATIONS	ENERGY FUNCTIONS
1	Groin (Base of Spine)	Primal Needs & Physical Existence
2	Abdomen (Ovaries & Testes)	Create & Nurture
3	Solar Plexus (Pancreas)	Need for Information & Power
4	Heart (& Thymus)	Need for Love & Compassion
5	Throat (Thyroid)	Need for Higher Wisdom
6	Third eye on Forehead (Pituitary)	Bridging of the Subtle Realms
7	Crown on top of head (Pineal)	Dissolution into the Essence of All or Spirit

[Source: Cyndi Dale, *The Subtle Body*, 2009]

Eckhart Tolle uses the feeling of the total subtle energy body as a point of focus rather than using the individual *chakras* for spiritual experiences. Your focus for meditation practices is your choice, since there are multiple doorways to the Divine.

Energy of the Love Age

An individual's energy fields affect the energy level of the collective consciousness. The higher the individual's energy vibrations are and the more people there are who have these higher levels, the higher the collective vibrations will be. This is what brings a consciousness of peace and love to the planet and it is what will manifest the Love Age. The *Kryon* books by Lee Carroll are filled with information about this increase in vibrations here on Earth and about the effect this vibrational increase has on helping to bring about a higher collective consciousness.

According to *Kryon*, the increase in the level of vibrations by humans has created a change in the vibrational frequency and the magnetic grid on Earth. This is where the collective energy of the planet is stored and also has an influence on the level of spiritual consciousness for humans. Science is also confirming this relationship between earth's vibrations and humans well being.

Worldwide, we are experiencing a new level of energy vibrations according to research by physicists that used the Schumann Resonance indicator for earth's frequency. The frequency had been at 7.8 Hz for a long time, but since 1980 it has been rising and is currently between 11 and 12 cycles per second.

Early flights of the astronauts found that when they went above the ionosphere layer surrounding earth where the 7.8 Hz vibrations did not exist, the astronauts had health problems. To solve the problem scientists had to develop a device to simulate the 7.8 Schumann waves. This plus other research of brain waves has indicated that there is a relationship between the health of humans and these Schumann waves as well as other possible effects. (www.earthbreathing.co.uk/sr.htm)

Scientists have also been telling us that the magnetic grids have been adjusting since the late 1980s and getting weaker. Professor Bannerjee of the University of New Mexico has estimated that this grid has lost about half of its intensity over the last 4,000 years. Some believe the north and south poles my flip-

Energy Fields and Spiritual Oneness

flop, but for the time being there seems to be a low probability of that happening,

With the earth's vibrations increasing and the magnetic grid weakening, there definitely seems to be a physical shift occurring. This seems to correspond to the shift in consciousness that is currently happening, which increases energy vibrations to make it easier for us to experience higher levels of spirituality. This will definitely help bring about more people experiencing oneness and the Love Age consciousness.

There are some areas where the magnetic energy allows for a greater access to higher spiritual vibrations and wisdom. One of the areas where this is occurring is on the West Coast of North America. I remember hearing Eckhart Tolle saying in a video that when he was in England, he was inwardly directed to move to the West Coast. He did not know why he was directed there. When he arrived in Vancouver, British Columbia, Canada, he sat at his kitchen table and wondered why he was there. He thought of returning to England, but he received the guidance that he should write a book. When he did this, it led to his groundbreaking insights into how his readers could increase their spiritual energy vibrations by living in the Now. Later, he realized that it was the energy on the West Coast that had helped him to write *The Power of Now*.

Lee Carroll is also located on the West Coast, in the San Diego area. I have come to believe that Carroll and Tolle are the foremost providers of information guiding us into the Love Age. Just before I did the final editing of the proof copy of this book, I read Neale Donald Walsch's book, *The Storm before the Calm* who is from Ashland, Oregon. I decided to add him to the list of West Coast authors providing information about the Love Age.

By the way, Tolle calls the Love Age the New Earth, while Carroll calls it the New Age or the New Jerusalem. Walsh believes we need to write a New Cultural Story, and you can help in this endeavor by accessing www.TheGlobalConversation.com.

I have been writing my book since 1998, but this began only after I left California to live in Minnesota. I often wondered why I left the West Coast after reading how other authors were positively affected by its vibrations. One of the possible reasons that I was directed to live in Minnesota was so I would be able to attend the Loft Literary Center to learn more about how to write. About twelve years after moving, I read a suggestion in one of *Kryon's* books that people should move to colder climates, and Minnesota sure qualified for that. Maybe the cold Minnesota winters freeze the ego for better access to divine wisdom.

After a time in Minnesota, before I knew any of the above information about the West Coast vibrations helping authors, my wife and I found a way to live in Minnesota during the summer and in California during the winter. This probably gave me the chance to tap into some of the West Coast energy, where my writing has been more effective and creative.

Both Tolle and *Kryon* have said that the new energy would be more stabilized by 2012, which would make it easier for people to become enlightened beings at a faster pace. My experiences of trying to be an enlightened being for some 74 years were slow and painful. I used to believe it would be impossible to increase the world's spiritual consciousness, since few would want to take the time or effort to do it. Since the turn of the century, however, I have observed the increase in my own level of spiritual experiences while writing this book. The level of these experiences has increased significantly in comparison to my earlier years, and it is speeding up at an ever-increasing pace.

I have also noticed the same pattern of faster spiritual unfoldment among the people I have had the privilege of being with in book discussions in Pennsylvania and California. They are spiritually unfolding and this has made me a believer in the increasing pace of spiritual unfoldment with the new energy and consciousness. *Kryon* had channeled that this is a gift we have earned as humans, and it will be easier to be dual citizens of the physical and spiritual dimensions as a result.

Energy Fields and Spiritual Oneness

I've become a believer in the idea that this is actually happening and that the Love Age has a greater probability of happening now than at any other time in history. Jesus and other spiritual giants tried to initiate it, but the consciousness of their time did not allow it. Today, the consciousness is much higher, and it is growing. I now believe it is my life's purpose to help make this shift in spiritual energy in order to help bring about the Love Age.

The shift from ego polarization to spiritual oneness is one of the shifts needed for the Love Age to be realized. Ego consciousness of "me vs. them" ignites conflicts and polarization, which is so easy to observe in today's political and economic relationships. We need the inner knowingness of oneness with all, which provides the underlying experience and guidance for living in unity and in cooperation with others.

Realizing the interconnectivity of energy fields emphasizes the commonness we have with other humans and with the other environments we interact with. We are interrelated and in unity at the quantum energy level, and we should not be in a dominating and controlling relationships with other energy fields. Working in cooperation and harmony with them is the way of love.

I have spent a lot of time on energy, but an understanding of energy is basic to the understanding of spirituality and love. Love in its purest form is energy, and it packs a powerhouse of tools for creating a better world for all. The next three chapters will discuss the shift from the good-for-me motivation to the good-for-All motivation.

Figure 6.2

> **SUGGESTED QUESTIONS FOR PERSONAL AND GROUP DISCUSSION**
>
> 1. Have you ever read a scientific study about energy fields that helped validate your spiritual experiences?
> 2. Have you experienced the power of love energy in your life?
> 3. Have you ever used *chakras* in your spiritual practices or for healing?
> 4. Have you noticed that the heightened energy on Earth has made it easier for your or for others' spiritual growth?
> 5. Have you experienced the energy power of your thoughts to co-create things, circumstances, or states of consciousness in your life?
> 6. Are you aware of how polarized the ego consciousness is in today's world?
> 7. Have you noticed how humans and the world are becoming more united even though there is increased polarization?

☺ *Smile* ☺
You're a powerful being of spiritual energy.
Are you using your energy to energize the world with love?

SHIFT III

Good-For-Me to Good-For-All

Most people who operate out of the ego consciousness desire to get either what is good-for-me or what is good-for-others. To be more loving, your intentions, motivations, and actions must arise out of what is good-for-All. Doing what's good-for-All is, in its essence, living a life based on divine love in all your relationships. Shifting from good-for-me to good-for-All motivations is the single most important shift for establishing the Love Age. It is a shift from the fear and conflict of the ego to love. Living and making decisions with divine love is the most important shift for changing yourself and the world. It is the motivating essence behind the Love Age.

Chapter Seven

Amanda Dream – Love's Turning Point

For the first four decades of my life, most of what I did or desired was a dilemma between two competing motivations. I wasn't sure whether I should desire things for the good-of-me or for the good-of-others.

In the late 1970s, I started experiencing a lot of mental, physical, and spiritual pain. I think of this period as the "dark night of soul," and all I wanted was relief from it. I pleaded that whatever lesson I had to learn, would it please quickly show itself? It was not until later in life that I realized these difficulties were a turning point for understanding one of the most important aspects of love. This was the most difficult time of my life as well as the most significant turning point in learning to be more loving.

Nomadic Life

From 1977 to 1979, my family and I accelerated our formerly slow nomadic pace of living. During this period, we moved from New Castle, Pennsylvania, where I taught sociology at Westminster College, to Phoenix, Arizona. Then we moved to Marianna, Pennsylvania (my hometown), back west to Boulder, Colorado, and back again to Marianna. After the children finished the school year, we had completed one year of nomadic moving. Our next move was to San Diego, California, for the summer months. In the fall we went back east to Hazard, Kentucky, where I taught in the University of Kentucky's Community College system for nine months before moving west again to Turlock, California. This made a grand total of nearly seven cross-country moves within a two-year period.

***

Years later when my grandson, Sean, studied nomads in a second- or third-grade social studies class, his teacher told them, "Nomads are a group of people who move a lot, but they always have one place they call home." Sean raised his hand, and the teacher said, "Sean, do you have a question?"

"No. But I think my mother was a nomad when she was young. Her family moved all over the United States, but their home was in Pennsylvania." There's a wise saying that out of the mouths of children, the truth shall be known. Sean accurately viewed his mother, BJ, as a teenage nomad.

***

During the first year of this nomadic period, I was unemployed and tried to decide what new career I should pursue. My ego believed a perfect job was somewhere out there. Also, my wife and I wanted to relocate our family of four children and two dogs, which was like chasing the ego illusion of Shangri-La.

The ego is good at constructing mental and emotional illusions that become unrealistic motivations and that create unhappiness when they are not realized. I'll let you in on a little secret about life. There is no perfect job or a Shangri-La in the ego state of consciousness; ego desires, at best, only create relative satisfaction, and most of the time, they create a lot of unhappiness. From a higher spiritual level of awareness, all of the difficult circumstances we find ourselves in are perfect since they are lessons we created for ourselves in order to become more enlightened beings.

Our family now laughs about these nomadic escapades. However, while living through them, I experienced emotional, mental, physical, and spiritual pain that made it seem as though we were traveling through the valley of the shadow of death.

This nomadic experience forced me to look at life at a deeper level, and it initiated one of life's most significant turning points. It helped to answer the basic question of **why** I should be spiritual in the first place. The motivations of my intentions and actions should be for the good-of-All, which is the same as living a life based on love rather than based on ego's fears, conflicts, and me centeredness.

One of the important aspects of life is to understand why you want or desire something, since motivations determine the consequences of your actions. When I observed the impact of my frequent moves on the family and especially the way in which they affected the children, I was in a dilemma about whether I should be living my life for the good-of-me or for the good-of-them. I knew it was right to want what was good-for-others, but how was I to realize my own desires?

> ***Actions Speak Nothing if You do Not Know the Motive***

Over time, I've learned that the reason why I do something is more important than the actions I take, since intentions are what initiate, direct actions, and attract the consequences I receive. It is important to be conscious of motivations, since awareness determines whether my choices are done with or without love. I have found that the more spiritual I become, the more I'm able to detect the true motivations of other people.

Amanda Literature Dream

I had a dream that gave me guidance about how to resolve my dilemma about wanting what's good-for-me versus what's good-for-others. About ten years before starting the intensive nomadic period of my life, I learned that my nightly dreams were important for helping me understand what was going on in my inner and outer lives. At that time, dreams were my primary doorway for receiving divine wisdom. I wrote my dreams down and diligently analyzed them for their hidden messages of wisdom. Surprisingly, a significant spiritual dream made its way through all the negativity I experienced during my "dark night of soul."

One evening after living in Boulder, Colorado, for several months, I was in bed and unable to go to sleep. My wife was already asleep. The night light in the hallway shone through the bedroom door and cast shadows off unpacked boxes of books and other household items. Negative thoughts about my six months of unemployment, job rejections, and financial problems occupied my mind. I felt a deep loneliness that stemmed from living in an uncaring and cruel world, where it even seemed the Divine had abandoned me. I was wondering if God had become a mute or maybe even had Alzheimer's and had forgotten about me.

> *Worries & Stress Are Ego's Garbage. Please, Empty Quickly.*

My ego self was on the defensive and reacted to all of the negative garbage I experienced. It dragged me down to one of the lowest victim states of consciousness that I had ever experienced. Tears intermittently ran down my cheek and onto the pillow. I kept my head turned from Audrey, my wife, in case she might awaken and see me.

Later that night, a glimmer of hope crept into my thoughts as I remembered receiving help from past dreams. I wondered if I could possibly receive help from a dream again. Before going to sleep that night, I halfheartedly begged, *Please show me what career is right for me and help me know what to do to find a job. Please!*

The next morning, as I awoke, I lay motionless in bed, since in the past this had always helped me to remember the details of dreams. After mentally reviewing last night's dream, I reached for my dream journal on the nightstand. Since I had to help get the children ready for school and had to fix breakfast, I had no time to waste. I hurriedly recorded the date and started writing key words to help me remember the dream's details to record later. I quickly wrote the following:

Marianna

African-American lady—classmate and coal miner

Coal miners and their wives' comments

Read Amanda Literature

As I went about my morning responsibilities, I pondered the meaning of the dream. The dream symbol of the African-American woman clearly had something to do with my job problems and with the Affirmative Action program. I felt disappointed. I wanted a dream to help me find a job rather than to remind me about my negative attitudes associated with job-hunting.

Why was I given this dream? It bothered me that I didn't have the foggiest idea about the meaning of the "Read Amanda Literature" command that I had heard as I awoke from the dream. *Why was the dream cloaked in obscure words and symbols when I needed a straightforward answer about getting a job?*

As I served eggs to my wife, I tried to keep these thoughts about the dream from distracting me. Audrey said, "I saw you writing in your dream journal this morning. Do you want to tell me about it?"

"I'm not sure what some of it means. It seems the first part dealt with minorities and Affirmative Action, but I'm thoroughly confused about the command given at the end of the dream."

"Maybe I can make some sense of it if you tell it to me," she said.

Our four children were also eating breakfast at the table, and they looked up at me. It appeared that they were interested in hearing it too. I paused and reluctantly began telling it.

"In the dream, I was walking from my parents' house along a street in Marianna. You know the one that goes past the old carpenter shanty building. I saw a female classmate who attended elementary and high school with me. She walked from her house to the sidewalk where I stood. I remember your family telling me that she was one of the women recently hired at the coal mine, but I don't remember anything we talked about.

As I continued to walk down the road toward the house where you grew up, I started to recall the things I heard coal miners and their wives saying about women who worked in the mines. Things like: It's unlucky to have a woman in the mines, they can't work like a man can, we're always doing extra work because of them, they're taking jobs from a man's family.

At this point the dream faded away and I was in a state of twilight sleep, where I couldn't see anything like I did in the visual part of the dream. I heard a male voice command me—Read Amanda Literature." I paused. "Before going to sleep last night, I asked for guidance for a new career and where I could find a job and this is what I got."

Audrey said, "I sure hope it doesn't mean you're going to be a coal miner."

"Me too," I nodded in agreement as she continued.

"But what's that Read Amanda Literature mean?"

"I wish I knew. If I understood it, I might know more about what the dream was trying to tell me."

My youngest daughter looked up at me from across the table, with her eyes just peering over her bowl and asked, "Daddy, when are you going to get a job?"

I looked down at the floor and said, "I hope soon, honey."

What Does Amanda Mean?

Weeks later, I was sitting alone at the kitchen table, since the children were at school and my wife was at work. I started to think about what I would cook for the family's evening meal. My thoughts wondered off, and I started to fear that I might end up being a househusband for the rest of my life. I thought about being unemployed and useless and being a victim of life's cruel circumstances. My ego felt deflated, as if life had thrown horse manure on me and was about to suffocate my stinky, worthless self.

I looked down at the linoleum floor and back up at the dark brown kitchen cabinets. As I aimlessly looked around, I noticed the beige wall matching the carpets. It seemed that every apartment I had ever lived in was painted this same color. These drab colors deepened my depression. Would I ever own another home and paint it with colors I liked? At that point, my thoughts took an abrupt turn, and I began to wonder about Amanda Literature and its meaning.

I couldn't remember "Amanda Literature" being mentioned in any of my college or graduate school classes. In some of my infrequent meditations during this period, I asked to know the meaning of Amanda Literature, but nothing came through. I also never heard it mentioned in any of the various religious paths I had pursued. My efforts to find its meaning were fruitless.

Out of nowhere, I had a vague intuitive impression that I should use the dictionary to find the meaning of the word, "Amanda." I pushed my chair back from the table and went into the bedroom to look through the unpacked boxes. After finding my old college dictionary, I went back to the table and opened it to find the word "Amanda."

I remembered that proper names were listed in the back part of that dictionary. When I found the word "Amanda," my eyes lit up in astonishment. Amanda meant—**Worthy to Be Loved.**

The dream seemed to be telling me to love those minorities who I thought were taking my jobs. They were the ones worthy to be loved.

Have you ever had a dream that helped you understand your life's experiences?

Later that evening, after everyone went to bed, I sat in the living room chair and began to think about how clever divine wisdom was in coming up with the word, Amanda, as a dream symbol. It was a female name that meant "worthy to be loved." It fit in perfectly with the emotional problems I struggled with concerning women now defined as minorities according to the newly legislated Affirmative Action program. My ego consciousness was sure that this was what had created my difficulties in finding a job.

The Amanda revelation also helped make me aware of the hidden resentments I had been internalizing. It informed me about my lack of love. This insight came through a back door via my dream, since the ego mind and emotions had closed every other door for receiving divine guidance. Regardless of my admiration for this dream wisdom, it was still difficult to swallow and was even harder to put into practice.

I realized that at a deeper unconscious level, I was consumed with anger about being a victim of my employment circumstances. This anger, a mental cancer, was closing off the flow of love into and out of my heart and was devouring what little love I had for others and myself.

The emotional energy of these anger cells had been increasing in strength as they consumed more and more of my heart. Any desire of mine to follow the dream's message about love was being effectively counteracted by volatile emotions. I was locked in a constant ego battle to protect what little was left of my ego's self-worth. It was a state of consciousness I did not like.

Anger Is Cancer Devouring Love & Destroying Relationships

At that time, I just didn't have the knowledge or tools I needed in order to know how to allow Soul to take charge and to make needed changes. The fear of financial doom, negative attitudes of self-worth, and pessimistic feelings of empowerment ruled my life. I was far from being a spiritual person, but I was about to learn one of life's most valuable lessons.

I knew that learning how to control my fears and attitudes while changing anger into love would take time. My desire to cleanse my heart and to replace those attitudes with more positive ones would create a soothing breeze of love flowing from within. If I could do this, it would open my heart to receive more love, and I would eventually be able to give it to others. An empty glass of water cannot quench another's thirst, just as a person empty of love cannot demonstrate love.

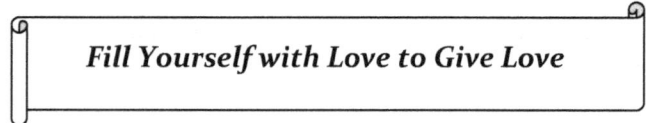

Fill Yourself with Love to Give Love

My first task was to try to fill myself with love in order to replace the anger. I felt grateful for learning what the name Amanda meant, but I was still puzzled about what "Read Amanda Literature" meant. Did it mean to read literature worthy to be loved, like good literature? Did it mean to read literature that deals with the topic of love? Did "Amanda Literature" actually exist? Fortunately, I was about to receive additional help and insights about the full meaning of "Read Amanda Literature."

What Does "Read Amanda Literature" Mean?

During one of my meditations when I pondered the meaning of Amanda Literature, I received an intuitive nudge about the book, *Stranger by the River*, by Paul Twitchell. The nudge seemed to suggest I should read the book again. I wasn't enthusiastic about that, but I eventually decided to follow this inner nudge, since experiences had taught me that I might otherwise miss a learning opportunity. Little did I expect this nudge would help lead to one of my life's most valuable insights.

Have you ever had an inner nudge that helped give you a valuable insight?

A third of the way through the book, my consciousness was reawakened to some of the basic principles about love that I hadn't been practicing. First, love is more than a belief or a feeling. It should be demonstrated. Another principle dealt with my desire to feel loved, especially by the world outside my immediate family. If I wanted to be loved, and I did, I needed to fill myself with love in order to give and receive it from others. Could this be why I was directed to read this book? The book helped focus my attention on some of the principles of love that I wasn't practicing, but I still felt empty in my heart. There had to be more.

A day or two later, I read the following sentence: "So do not desire that for others which you do not desire for [yourself]... " I thought. This was what Audrey and I had been talking about concerning the dilemma of our children's desires and ours. As I continued to read, I experienced an additional insight: "Take the short cut to God and give of [yourself]...to all." This sentence jolted my consciousness. I put the book down to reflect on its meaning.

Them versus Me Dilemma

When I was a teenager, my church taught that the ultimate expression of love was to sacrifice myself for the ***good-of-others.*** This was deeply embedded in my consciousness. This new idea of desiring the same for myself as for others was different. I had always thought that if I sacrificed myself for others' good, I would be practicing the highest form of love.

I knew that wanting what's good-for-others was right, but wanting what's ***good-for-me*** was selfishness or downright greed. Wanting something for just me was a no-no. I was always in a dilemma when I wanted something in life for myself, especially when it was in conflict with others' desires for the same thing. These experiences created inner turmoil, especially when I acted for the good-of-me. Over the years, the inner turmoil accumulated into a heavy load of guilt about being selfish. It felt as though I was carrying around a ten-ton bag of guilt.

I wondered. *If I desired what was good-for-others, how would I ever get a job? Did I want others to get jobs I wanted? No, I didn't. I had a family to support.* I grew up with the ego working-class value that the man supported the family. Since I was unemployed, my ego's self-worth had taken a hard hit.

I continued thinking. *I had just read that I should desire the same for me that I desire for others. Was this desiring in fact the same as doing what was good-for-All? If so, how was it done?*

I had interpreted reality according to the beliefs and experiences of my good-for-others consciousness, but this interpretation wasn't working. I was not the one receiving the good stuff. I wondered if doing what was good-for-All might resolve my dilemma of "them versus me." The "them vs. me" was how my ego differentiated itself from others. My ego viewed others as separate, and it used conflict to maintain this separation. In contrast, the good-for-All view was based on unity and oneness where relationships were built on love and cooperation for the greater good-of-All.

This new good-for-All option suggested that I should desire the same good for myself as I would for others. I thought that if I accepted this, I would be on an equal footing with others. If I then desired a job others wanted, I would not have to feel guilty about including myself.

I gradually understood that the all not only included others whom my life touched, but the *all also included me.* At last, I did not feel I should be excluded from desiring what was good in life, and this gave me an inner freedom from the feelings of selfishness and guilt. Finally, I knew that I was to include myself as well as others when desiring something good.

Those who are deeply immersed in the ego self with its desire for the good-of-me could easily misinterpret the meaning of the above paragraph. It is saying that the inclusion of yourself as an equal in relationships with others is what's good, but it's not suggesting an unequal desiring or receiving, which is what's good-for-me. It's a difficult balance to know what good-for-All is, and we will see in a coming chapter that it takes wisdom greater than what our rational minds can grasp. That is why the good-for-All relationship requires a different approach for finding spiritual solutions for life's difficulties.

Desiring and Doing What's Good-for-All Includes Me Too

About a week or so after that initial revelation, I was still pondering the meaning of good-for-All. It was as if I had walked into another room of my consciousness and had turned on a light switch, only to discover that there were other rooms to explore in order to understand love.

I knew that from then on, when I wanted something in life, I should desire what's *good-for-All*. This would be my main motivation in life for whatever desires or intentions I might have. Finally, I could freely and knowingly use my desires in a relationship with those who wanted the same things I did. This realization would now serve as my new inner guidance system, just like the GPS device in automobiles that guided me along streets and highways.

The realization of this new value of doing and desiring what's good-for-All was a major turning point, and it created a shift in my ego consciousness.

Do you desire what's good-for-All in your life?

Arriving at this realization was a gradual process, but the application of the realization proved to be an even slower process. Fortunately, the "them **or** me" dilemma was resolved by desiring the good in life for them **and** for me—that is, for the all.

Am I Amanda Too?

One evening, as I lay awake in bed, I thought, *I know Audrey loves me, and I love her as well as our children. I knew our children loved us, though they were not pleased with the moves that had resulted in lost friends. Even during times of family conflict, the children had maintained kind and respectful family* relationships, and most of the time, they had graciously accepted the difficulties.

This told me that despite our differences, they still loved me. They were not nomadic brats but were children with loving and kind hearts. I'm proud of how my children matured in life, despite the hard times they experienced. However, I knew I still had a lesson to learn about how to love myself just as my family loved me.

Good-for-All

The ego self reacts like a robot,
  Looking for the good-for-me jackpot.

Sometimes the ego works in disguise,
  Sacrificing to maximize the other's prize.

Doing good-for-All is for the wise,
  Equalizing and making love harmonize.

I was thankful for the kindness and heartfelt love I received from my family. It provided a life jacket with enough affection to help me keep my head above the negative cesspool of anger festering within until I could eventually learn to love others and myself.

Throughout my life, the issue of loving myself bothered me. What exactly was it like to love myself? Where did vanity stop and the love of self begin? With only vague answers to these questions, I did know that love flowed only from those who were filled with it and that to be filled with love, one had to love one's self.

I knew I had to find ways to regenerate the love that my cancerous anger and fears had devoured. This would help open my consciousness to allow love to flow to others, while the return flow would help replenish my own heart. This giving and receiving of love was needed in order to put what's good-for-all into practice.

> ***Loving Yourself Helps Soul Fill Your Heart with Love for Others, You, and the Divine***

I eventually realized that "Amanda," which meant worthy to be loved, didn't just apply to minorities, but that I was worthy of love too. If I didn't love myself, I wouldn't be able to love others. It was that simple.

Do you love yourself???

I'm not sure how many years it was after the "Read Amanda Literature" dream that I was able to relate the dream to what Jesus said about love. He said, "Love your neighbor **as** yourself." He did not say love your neighbor **less than** yourself (good-for-me). He also didn't say love your neighbors **more than** yourself (good-for-others). Good-for-All love was to be given in equal portions for both oneself and others.

> ***Good-for-All Love Equalizes Life's Good***

It was a difficult purification process to turn the cesspool of negativity in my consciousness into the loving of others and of myself. I had to learn to be conscious of moments when my thoughts were not of a loving nature, so I could replace them with thoughts in harmony with love. I also learned to live more in the presence of the Divine and its love derived from within. I took small steps to eventually fill myself with the sparkling water of pure divine love, so I could be a channel for what's good-for-All.

Eventually I learned that it wasn't the love of the ego or the body that was the target of self-love, it was instead Soul. Soul is the true self. Under the ego consciousness, I use to love myself or feel more worthy if I had worldly success or achievements that society held in high esteem. This rarely happened and when it did, it was of a temporary nature. I therefore didn't have much love for myself until I directed my self-love toward Soul. Loving Soul was the one thing that put love into my heart since I not only loved my true self, but loved the Divine at the same time.

It does not mean that I do not love the ego since hating it would be a reaction that would further my attraction to that consciousness. Instead it is a love that is based on being detached from result of my desires for social rewards as well as respect for the positive mental functions of the mind.

I realize now that the "Amanda" dream was a turning point and was given to teach me how to be a more spiritual being of love. Since love is the greatest power in the world for peace, joy, and harmony, living a life of love will give you the power needed to live that life. When you intend something in your life, always desire it for the good-of-All. When you act to realize your intentions, always do them for the good-of-All too. This is how a spiritual person of love lives.

Figure 7.1

> **SUGGESTED QUESTIONS FOR PERSONAL AND GROUP DISCUSSION**
> 1. Have you ever had an experience that taught you something about love?
> 2. Have you ever had a "dark night of soul" experience where you felt abandoned by the Divine and were at one of the lowest points of your life?
> 3. Did you learn anything from this "dark night of soul" experience?
> 4. Have you ever had a dream that gave you guidance?
> 5. Have you ever been in a dilemma about whether you should desire what's good for yourself or others?
> 6. Do you feel worthy to be loved?
> 7. How does your ego block love from being received and given?
> 8. Has anger ever eaten love out of your heart like a cancerous cell eats healthy cells in your body?
> 9. Do you fill yourself with love to be able to give love?
> 10. Do you mostly operate out of being good-for-me, good-for-others, or good-for-All?
> 11. Have you had an experience where you put good-for-All desires and actions into practice?
> 12. Do you want the power of love?

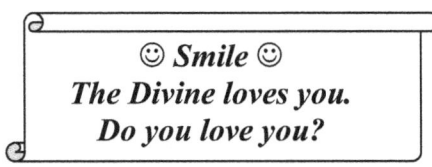

☺ *Smile* ☺
The Divine loves you.
Do you love you?

Chapter Eight

Is Win/Win the Same as Good-for-All?

When I was in a discussion group talking about the good-for-All principle, a woman asked me, "Is good-for-All like win/win in psychology?"

What do you think?

Good-for-All is similar to win/win but with an important difference. Win/win is based on the conflicting relationships of winning or losing, which is part of the ego conflict state of consciousness. The ego self uses mental judgments, willpower, logic, compromises, and reasoning to resolve conflicts. It tries to determine the best mental compromise for equally distributing winnings, yet without the all-encompassing view of divine wisdom. In a win/win compromise there is still some degree of losing, but it is better than doing what is good-for-me.

On the other hand, good-for-All is based on divine wisdom from a higher source that absolutely knows what's best for All. It derives from a consciousness of higher wisdom as well as of cooperation and love. Instead of relying on the ego reasoning of the mind for a solution, the Divine uses us as channels to manifest divine wisdom for the greater good. It's a higher, more compassionate, and encompassing wisdom that knows what's best for all, especially when we want something that others also want. Divine wisdom knows what's good for others, for me, and for the divine purpose, but the ego mind doesn't.

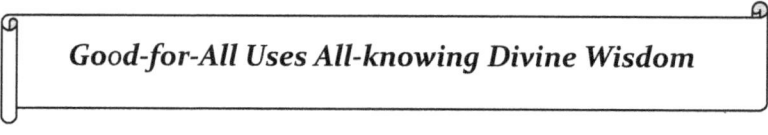

Good-for-All Uses All-knowing Divine Wisdom

***

At first, I too thought that good-for-All was the same thing as a win/win solution. I was sincerely trying to use my rational thoughts when I searched for a new career that would be a win/win situation for my children, for my wife, for others, for my employer, and to some extent for me.

After leaving my teaching position at Westminster College in 1977 and starting the accelerated nomadic life, I had a vague idea about what new career to pursue. I thought there might be two possibilities. When I had worked as a carpenter in the past, I felt creative. Therefore, I thought that being a construction contractor might be an interesting career. I also perceived myself as a people person, and I thought that I might want to help others by being a marriage, family, and child counselor.

To qualify for either of these careers would take additional experience and education, and I wondered how I could afford to acquire either while still trying to support my family. In addition to the insecurity of the two career choices requiring additional skills, I was overwhelmed by financial fears. Experiencing these conflicting negative thoughts and fears was not a good way to start searching for new employment. Also, my confusion about which career to pursue also confused the Divine Energy about my intentions.

Is Win/win the Same as Good-for-All?

Even though I desired a win/win outcome for a new career, my ego fears had taken over the decision making process. Instead of actively looking for a new career, I decided to backslide into my old career of teaching sociology or doing social research.

Choosing not to make a career change seemed more comforting than facing the fears and insecurities of learning a new one. But even this coward's way out ran into difficulties when my applications for teaching positions were counteracted by the Affirmative Action laws. In addition, when I applied for college positions in California, the newly passed Proposition 13 threatened to reduce tax funding for higher education. Consequently, California colleges were not hiring, and this, too, became a roadblock for returning to my old career. It seemed roadblocks were placed at every turn when I wanted to return to my old career. The Divine was pushing me hard to go into another career, despite my fears.

While I had supported the Affirmative Action program initially, my attitude had changed when I became personally affected by it. My anger increased, and I felt I was a victim of reverse prejudice. I was unconsciously internalizing this victim anger, which conflicted with my beliefs about the good of affirmative action.

After a year of unemployment, I spent a summer working as a carpenter in San Diego. I wasn't making much since I was paid by piece work and wasn't a fast-paced carpenter, so when an opportunity opened for a college teaching position in Hazard, Kentucky, I considered it. I can remember the terrible negative feeling I had in the pit of my stomach when I signed the contract. I resisted the intuitive message of guidance, and I signed the contract out of financial fear. Ego fears controlled my decision.

I didn't know at the time how my ego fears were directing my life. It wasn't rational to make a lot of long distant moves as we did in a two-year span or to move without the assurance of employment or housing waiting for us. As I look back now, I can see how the fears pushed my ego buttons to make me behave irrationally. The win/win solution was not working well.

Some of the ego fears I was dealing with during the highly paced nomadic life in the latter part of 1970s were the following:

- Fear of not finding a job.
- Fear that I would never know what my new career should be.
- Fear of losing what few material things we had packed in the pickup truck and trailer. (During the first move to Phoenix, the trailer broke away from the truck, which is a story of a miracle to be told at another time.)
- Fear that the overloaded truck would not make it to the next destination. I burned out a clutch once, and the head mechanic said that if I had the truck filled with feathers, it would have weighed too much.
- Fear that I was hurting the children.
- Fear that I would never own another home.
- Fear that I would never gain my self-worth.
- Fear that the Divine had abandoned me.
- Fear that the lack of health insurance would create problems when I tried to pay for treatment of my ulcer or for any other family medical bills that might arise.
- Fear that I would become homeless and would not be able to find an apartment, at the next destination, that accepted four children and two dogs.

If you were to ask me why we did what we did, I would have to say that my ego fears made me do it. It's similar to believing that "the devil made me do it."

Have you ever seen the old TV program, "Have Gun, Will Travel"? I saw a sign on an owner operated semitruck that said, "Have Bills Must Travel." When I saw this sign while traveling in

Is Win/win the Same as Good-for-All?

my pickup, I thought that I should put a sign on my truck that read, "Have Wife, Must Travel." But I didn't.

Figure 8.1

My wife received intuitive insights, especially when she did dishes, and they were usually about moving to some other place. This was what initiated many of our trips, and my ego blamed her for our nomadic life. Our family should have made a rule that Mom was not allowed to do dishes, which would have saved many nomadic miles.

Now, when I look back on the nomadic life, I realize that many of her intuitive insights were good for the family, so her intuition wasn't really at fault. Many years later, when I finally had nothing else to blame, I realized my ego fears were what controlled that erratic time of our life. The hard part to accept was that I was the one responsible for my own circumstances.

If I had been more spiritually evolved at that time, I would have been aware of the ego reacting because of my fears. Instead of reacting, I would have accepted the situation and replaced fears with solutions of love. To do this, I would have had to allow divine love to enter my state of consciousness in order to be open to good-for-All solutions. Although it took time, I feel fortunate that these negative circumstances eventually helped me become a better loving person.

***

Love Finds a Way While the Ego Finds Excuses

After teaching for a year in Kentucky, I tried carpentry again. When the housing market plummeted in California sometime around 1980, I was laid off. It was then that I decided to try to become a marriage, family, and child counselor. To be certified, I worked at a group home for teenagers who were having mental and emotional problems. They were not serious enough to be institutionalized in a mental hospital, but they had too many problems to allow them to live with their families.

One day at the group home, some of the staff and I were having a group counseling session with the residents. About a

Is Win/win the Same as Good-for-All?

half hour into the session, I heard the loud piercing sound of Divine Energy pouring through me. I had heard this familiar sound before. It was so loud that I was sure the others could hear it, but there were no signs that they did. I knew from experience that this was the way the Divine used me to channel love, wisdom, or whatever was needed for others or me. I wondered who in the group was getting the benefit of this divine sound.

A knock on the door jolted my mind's search for an answer. The staff person told me that I had a phone call in the office. When I answered the phone, it was my friend from Los Angeles. We had been classmates at the University of Pittsburgh in the graduate school of sociology, and he was working at the headquarters of the Children's Home Society of California. He asked me, "Would you be interested in moving to Los Angeles and working at the headquarters as a computer systems analyst and doing some social research for my department?"

I didn't answer right away, since all kinds of thoughts were going through my head. I thought, *Neither Audrey nor I liked living in large cities and especially Los Angeles, which is probably the gridlock capital of the world. Besides, I'm a people person, and I don't want to work with impersonal computers. I also don't know much about computers. I don't like moving the two youngest children to another school and putting the family through another move.*

When I finally answered my friend on the other end of the line, I tried to find the right words to say, "That sounds like a good job offer, but I'm not sure how the family will feel about moving to LA. I'm also not sure I would be qualified for the job, since I didn't do much computer work at Pitt or Westminster College."

"That's not a problem. We'll train you."

"That sounds good, but I will have to talk with my family and let you know."

"That's fine. I would sure like to work with you again."

"I feel the same way too."

When I talked to my wife, neither of us wanted to move to Los Angeles. The two youngest children sure didn't want to move either. As for myself, I wouldn't mind the research part of the position, but I wouldn't like the computer side of it. We initially thought that a win/win solution was to reject the job offer, but we decided to turn it over to the Divine for guidance. I also asked for guidance in meditation. Nothing came through, except at times, I would hear the presence of the inner sound as I went about my daily activities. I wondered what it was trying to tell me. When I thought about the job, I had a good feeling inside or heard the comfort of the inner sound.

These experiences were in conflict with my negative ego thoughts about the job. The ego self was reacting negatively, but the Divine guidance seemed to indicate that it was the thing to do. Fortunately, Audrey felt the same way, so we decided to accept the position, even though our egos and rational thoughts were telling us otherwise. Again, the win/win mental solution wasn't the decision that the Divine guided us to do.

If we had continued to focus our attention on the rational mind and our ego fears in order to find a win/win solution, we would not have made a decision to take the offer. Fortunately, we turned to the Divine for guidance, and we trusted that we were receiving the good-for-all solution.

***

I had been working at the group home for less than a year. Eventually, I ruled out counseling as a career option just as I had ruled out carpentry, but at least I had taken the actions necessary to evaluate the two careers. The process of elimination is sometimes the way decisions are made. At least I had tried them, to see if I wanted them.

The Divine guided me to a career that was good-for-All, even though I resisted it. After the Children's Home Society of California position, I worked for Martin Marietta Aerospace

Is Win/win the Same as Good-for-All?

Company as a financial computer systems analyst. This company was responsible for building the launch pad at Vandenberg Air Force Base (AFB) in California that would launch the space Shuttle into a north and south orbit around Earth. I also worked for Grumman Technical Services, who were responsible for running and maintaining the computers that would launch the Space Shuttle.

When the first space shuttle exploded and killed all who were on board, the Space Shuttle program was mothballed at Vandenberg AFB. After being unemployed for a while, I worked as a computer teacher and computer systems or research analyst for the State of California in the Department of Corrections, the Department of Justice, and the Integrated Waste Management Board. These jobs lasted until I retired.

Developing computer systems gave me a feeling of being creative. I did projects for departments that needed manual systems automated. Contrary to my belief about computer work being impersonal, I found as an analyst that most of my interactions were with people. I had to interview them to determine their needs and desires for a new computer system as well as to train them to use it. Being a computer systems analyst also used one of my strongest skills of analyzing data and information. As it turned out, it was the best career for my employers, my family, and me. That's how wise the Divine was, to lead me to a career that I initially resisted.

Good-for-All wisdom from the Divine is far superior to the limited knowledge of rationally derived win/win solutions. After repeated experiences of realizing that the limitations of the ego's rational mind did not provide good-for-All guidance, I gradually turned my attention to receiving more and more guidance from the Divine in everyday circumstances.

Figure 8.2

> **SUGGESTED QUESTIONS FOR PERSONAL AND GROUP DISCUSSION**
> 1. Have you tried to use win/win solutions?
> 2. Have you ever heard the inner sound of the Divine flowing through you to give guidance, peace, and love, or to feel this blessing of the Divine's energy?
> 3. Have you ever made a decision to do something when your ego or rational mind said "NO," but your inner guidance said "YES?"

☺ *Smile* ☺
You do not have to find win/win solutions.
*The Divine will let you know what is good-for-**All**.*

Chapter Nine

Is Love All You Need?

After I had the "Amanda" dream experience, I sought answers to the following questions. What is it like to live with love? Is doing what is good-for-All divine love? When am I demonstrating divine love in relationships with others? Is love all that is needed?

Is love doing what is good-for-All? There are various forms of love, and one of them is romantic love. Most people recognize this kind of emotional, sometimes blind love, since the media popularizes it and since it's usually the reason for marrying or divorcing someone. Even five-year-olds have opinions about it, which I read about on the Internet.

***

Karl was asked, "What does love mean?" He said, "Love is when a girl puts on perfume and a boy puts on shaving stuff and they go out and smell each other." Leave it to children to know the essence of romantic love. I saw a TV documentary on research about how the smell of pheromones given off by males attracted females, so Karl seemed close to the truth.

***

As a teenager, I concentrated on sacrificial love (good-for-others) as taught by the church. As stated before, the "Amanda" dream became the first significant turning point in my understanding of divine love, which gradually ignited other insights.

For example, one evening in Boulder, I was thinking about the meaning of the "Amanda" dream. I wondered, *What does good-for-All really mean?* I decided to do a spiritual meditation to try to receive an answer. Eventually, a subtle insight gently settled into my consciousness. *If you desire and do what's good-for-All, you demonstrate divine love.* It was a knowingness that came from a place deep within. I did not know how I knew it; I just knew it!

> ### *Doing Good-for-All Equals Divine Love and Vice Versa*

Why hadn't I realized this before? It was such a simple truth. When I realized that doing good-for-All was divine love, it helped make life more purposeful. I had finally solved one of my longtime confusions about love. I knew now that if I desired or did something in life with all my heart, for the good-of-All, I would indeed demonstrate divine love.

***

I later came to realize that the Divine also co-creates by doing what is good-for-All. Just imagine, if you remove one "o" from the word "good," you have God-for-All. The Divine truly creates for the good-of-All. The Divine has an overview of a situation that humans do not. It knows all of the possible future options and the effects that our intentions, motivations, or actions have on others, and it knows and does what's best for all if we desire and allow it.

I knew intentions affected others, my relationships with the Divine, and the lessons I would receive. On the other hand,

Is Love All You Need?

Divine Energy, being all-knowing, knew the specific potentials of my intentions and actions. This was why I knew that I must allow the Divine to guide my intentions and actions as well as allow it to co-create the what, how, when, and where of my intentions.

When I consciously co-created with the Divine, it took my desires and evaluated whether they were in harmony with the good-for-All. If they were in harmony with divine love, I would be guided to know how to help co-create it. The Divine often revises my desires and co-creates something better, or it adds a lesson or two for my spiritual development. If I allow it, the Divine always co-creates for the greater good. When I desire the good-for-All and put it into practice, I harmonize with and channel divine love.

What is the Higher Good?

In the physical world of the ego consciousness, circumstances are perceived as good or bad. It is a subjective assessment we engage in as we live in the world of opposites. During the years 1977 through 1979, I was filled with fears of financial doom and unworthiness, I was angered about Affirmative Action and unemployment, I felt that I was the victim of an uncaring world and was abandoned by God, and I experienced other ego fears. I was in a downward turn of life's cycles. My ego saw no help in these situations until I realized the importance of desiring and doing what's good-for-All.

An ego's eyes never see good in difficult circumstances. It takes a higher state of consciousness associated with living in the presence of the Divine to realize the good in difficulties, which are actually opportunities for learning love and experiencing a higher good. When I was unemployed for a year, I wondered how this could have any good in it. I didn't realize the good in my difficulties until years later, when soul's eyes were open.

I began to understand that my suffering was used in order to awaken my numbed ego consciousness to the importance of doing what's good-for-All. It was one of my greatest lessons learned in life. From the ego's perspective, it was a period filled with a lot of pain and suffering, the "baddest" of all the bad cycles I ever experienced.

How we perceive circumstances is important. The comedian, Jere Moormon, defined circumstances as "Latin for the mess we're in." Circumstances are a mess, according to the ego's eyes, but messes usually have in them a potential good or a gift for learning how to become more loving.

Doing what was good-for-All became my primary motivation for making love-based decisions. The hardships I experienced were well worth the lessons gained. This wisdom helped raise my limited understanding from an ego perspective to one where I could more easily detect the good hidden within difficult circumstances. I began to realize that the Divine worked behind the ego illusions and manifested what was good-for-All.

The word "All" points to a more encompassing meaning of good than what is just good-for-me or for another person. It also includes the Divine that uses us as channels to co-create what's best for all others, for all life, for me, and for the planet, as well as for the Divine's purpose and plans for our lives.

The "All" is more inclusive and puts us in harmony with the divine law of love. It is more than just what's good for the outer physical existence of humans, but it also includes what is good for inner spiritual unfoldment and for the divine's purpose. Using good-for-All broadens the field of what our intentions and actions affect.

> *Every Difficulty Has a Higher Good Hidden Within*

Is Love All You Need?

Desire and Do What Is Good-for-All

Co-creating is a tool whose use is motivated by love for the purpose of consciously changing yourself in a partnership with the Divine. Whenever there is something I desire or whenever a solution is needed, I make a request of divine wisdom to let me know what is good-for-All. I also request that my actions be done for the good-of-All. This is the purest of intentions. Only then can I open my heart and my soul's eyes to the subtle messages of divine guidance and love.

> *Good-for-All Intentions Are True Spirituality*

It is my hope that your most important motivation for consciously being spiritual will be based on love rather than on just for what is good-for-me or on some ego-based material or social success. These ego desires have their place, but they are secondary in significance to desiring the good-for-All. This is the way you can turn ego desires for a job, a loved one, a car, or a house into decisions made out of divine love. You can desire these things, but if you seek them, you should also add that you want them for the good-of-All. Desiring and doing what is good-for-All should be one's primary motivation for receiving earthly things or for spiritual growth.

> *Your Action Speaks Nothing Unless it is Motivated for the Good-of-All*

Instead of using the phrase good-for-All, you might be more comfortable stating it in another way. For example, you could say, "I want to give unconditional service or love to All, to do God's will, to walk in Jesus's footsteps, to love my neighbor as myself, or to do to others as I want them to do to me." You might also ask divine wisdom, "What do you want me to do now for the good-of-All? You could turn these into affirmations or inner talking as you go about your daily activities or when consciously trying to co-create something in your life.

As I said before, good-for-All served as my inner GPS guidance system, yet was more subtle and more difficult to follow than the woman's voice on my GPS. I wondered why they used a woman's voice on my GPS since I found throughout my life that I usually ran into difficulty if I followed my wife's directions while driving. I have to admit that she has gotten much better and can now understand north, south, east, and west on a map.

Even though it takes more consciousness to tune into divine guidance, that divine guidance has always been a better and more direct guide for the good-of-All than my ego consciousness has been. I also learned that when I based my inner guidance system on the good-for-All value, my life was propelled and guided with love. Since that's what I truly wanted, this goal became the cornerstone and motivation for life.

Love Desires and Does What Is Good-for-All

I now have a deeper appreciation for what the "Amanda" dream meant and for how pain acted as the primary motivator for learning it. The dream helped to establish a solid foundation that allowed me to be a co-creator and to do it with love. A higher good was subtly hidden behind the difficult circumstances I was experiencing in life. Divine love was what set me free from ego's control, and the lessons learned were worth a zillion times the pain endured.

My realization of good-for-All was not the kind of turning point where, in the next moment, I became a completely different person. It has been over 30 years since I had the "Amanda" dream, and the learning process is still going on. My journey made small, gradual changes, and it will most likely be a lifelong marathon without a finish line in sight. I have heard that the Divine works slowly, but when it comes to my spiritual growth, I've been moving at a sloth's pace for most of my life, until recently.

LOVE SETS YOU FREE

Choices have consequences, you must agree,
  Making Life's circumstances what they will be.

Ego fears, habits, and jealousies,
  Limit freedom like electronic devices on parolees.

While love's the key that sets you free,
  It's how divine trainees receive graduate degrees.

The significance of my shifts in consciousness went almost unnoticed until later in life. It was like walking on a moonlit beach and not being aware of the slow rising tide until I felt it between my toes. Important realizations tend to sneak subtly into my consciousness rather than coming in via earth-shaking experiences or with the blowing of trumpets.

All You Need Is Love

The Divine Source is the origin of divine love, Soul is that love, and our purpose in life is to use the love to co-create for the greater good. Divine Energy is divine love flowing from the Divine Source. When we live in divine presence, we receive messages of guidance, and we feel divine love as a heightened feeling of inner joy and peace. Divine love can also be experienced in the form of inner light and sound. If you see the inner light or hear the sound, this is an experience of divine love.

Have you ever experienced the inner light or sound?

The light that blinded St. Paul on the road to Damascus filled his heart with love for Christians, replacing the hatred he had once had for them. Experiencing these divine manifestations lets you know that the Divine is using you as a channel for divine love. But this was not the only way divine love appeared or communicated with me in my life, a subject that will be discussed more fully in another book. For love to manifest in our outer lives, we must consciously choose it and demonstrate it with actions.

I'm Soul; I'm Love

***

We sometimes receive the Divine's love spontaneously, as my wife did. One evening in 1969 or 1970, Audrey watched Billy Graham on television. She felt disturbed about his message of our being sinners, needing forgiveness and in need of salvation. She said, "Please God, help me know the truth." In an instant, she transcended her physical existence and experienced the love, peace, and joy of the Divine that surpassed all understanding. All she could say to describe it in words was, "I felt the love of God."

***

The truth is that the Divine is not wrathful and is not to be feared, and we are not sinners needing to feel guilty because Jesus was crucified some 2,000 years ago. This was church dogma added long after Jesus's death, to try to make sense of why the son of God was killed as a young man and in such a cruel way. The truth is that the Divine is love and we are to love the Divine, the Divine in us as Soul, and to love others, even our enemies. Love is all you need.

Life is Love and All the Rest Is Fluff

I'm realizing more and more that love is at the root of all I am and all I should do in life. Love others. Love my work. Love family. Love animals. Love God. Love myself. Love life. Love nature. Love all things. It's like the Beatles song, "All You Need Is Love." Life's main purpose boils down to this. I've found that the major lesson is learning love from life's difficulties. Consequently, it has become my primary purpose and motivation for living a life based on love.

Jesus and Love

When I was a teenager, I was introduced to Jesus's teachings of love, though I didn't see his teachings practiced much by church members. There seemed to be more ego wars going on between members of the church than there were conflicts in the world. I also didn't understand much about how to put Jesus's love into practice. I always thought that meant doing what was good-for-others (sacrificial love). It took me about another 24 years to have my next major understanding, which was initiated by the "Amanda" dream.

The ironic part of all of this was that Jesus taught about divine love and good-for-All when I was a teenager, but it took years to understand his gift. I went through a lot of hard knocks and pain to eventually make a full circle back to understand what Jesus taught about love.

There are three basic teachings of Jesus that are the basis for what I call divine love:

- *"Love the Lord your God with all your heart...soul, and...mind. This is the greatest and first commandment."* By loving the Divine, your heart opens to divine love and fills you with it. When I desire something to be for the good-of-All, I am filled with love for the Divine. Otherwise, I would be trying to get pure water out of an empty bottle. Don't forget that loving yourself as Soul is love of the Divine too.

Do you love the Divine?

> **Love Is Both the Oil That Runs Life Smoothly And the Glue Uniting Us in Peace & Harmony**

- *"You shall love your neighbor as yourself."* This is the best example of good-for-All love, rather than of the good-for-other love that the church taught me. It's loving everything equally and loving All.

Do you love yourself as well as your neighbor?

- *"You have heard that it is said, 'You shall love your neighbor and hate your enemies.' But I say to you, love your enemies..."* Wow! If you want your love to be for the good-of-All, just include your enemies. This is the part of the "All" that most people do not want to include in the practice of love.

Do you love those who intend to harm you or those who disagree with you?

Is Love All You Need?

> *If You Love Your Enemies, You'll Have No Enemies*

Love establishes a firm foundation for life. Co-creating with love will improve not only your individual state of consciousness and your life, but it will also help change the collective consciousness. The next three chapters will discuss the shift from ego-creating to LoveAge-creating.

Figure 9.3

SUGGESTED QUESTIONS FOR PERSONAL AND GROUP DISCUSSION
1. Have you ever had an experience where you did something for the good-of-all and felt the love?
2. Can you remember an experience where the ego saw only bad in a situation, but later you realized a lesson, understanding, or something positive from a difficulty?
3. Have you ever experienced how divine wisdom guided you to do what was best for All?
4. At what pace has your spiritual growth been progressing? (Snails? Walking? Jogging? Or Running?)
5. Would you agree that "All You Need Is Love"?

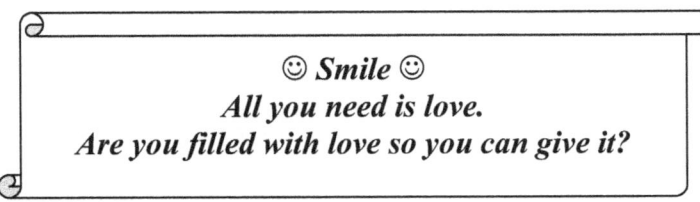

☺ *Smile* ☺
All you need is love.
Are you filled with love so you can give it?

Your Creative Power of Love

SHIFT IV

Ego-creating to LoveAge-creating

What are the major ways in which people create their personal and social circumstances? I found that my earlier life progressed through two ego-creating phases, which included me-creating and other-creating. In the transitional phase, I experienced ego-realization and soul-realization, which helped in recognizing ego habits and knowing myself as Soul. When I shifted into LoveAge-creating, I became a co-creator with the Divine while continuing to learn the power of oneness-creating.

These phases are mental constructions based on my life's experiences while trying to create my own personal destination as well as trying to help change society. You may not have the same creative journey of learning as I did. I hope the construction of these phases helps you understand your own creative powers and what you might want to focus on for changing your life.

Shifting from ego-creating to LoveAge-creating heightens your love and power to make good-for-All changes. You will create a blessed life for yourself as well as increasing the probability of creating the Love Age where peace, freedom, happiness, and love fill the world. Co-creating and oneness-creating are the ways for conscious change in the twenty-first century.

Chapter Ten

Ego-creating Phases

In some way or another, anyone who is in the ego-creating phase considers himself or herself a victim of random forces. Many view themselves as victims of other people, of their life's circumstances, or of the random forces of luck, chance, or God's wrath. Sometimes these people do strange things to influence the roll of life's dice. My grandmother, for example, had a strange way of creating good luck for bingo.

***

When I was eight or nine years old, my mother, brothers, and I visited my grandparents' apartment. I stood next to my mother in the kitchen listening to her talk to grandma, who was sitting on a maroon cushion that looked too large for a kitchen chair. I asked, "Why is your cushion so big, Grandma?"

"It's filled with horse manure. I'm sitting on it so I'll have good luck for bingo tonight."

"Are you going to take it to bingo?"

"Sure am. It's going to win me a lot of money."

"How did you get manure in it? Wasn't it sloppy and stinky?"

"It's dried manure, honey, but you have to make sure it's horse manure and not from cows. I wrapped it good. Put padding over it and sewed on the cover. I know another woman who does this, and she's always lucky at bingo."

I didn't say any more, but I thought to myself, *I'd never do that to get good luck*. By the way, I never observed any improvement in her financial status, so you might not want to try a horse manure pillow for good luck.

***

Me-creating and other-creating are the two phases of ego-creating. Both are under the direction and control of the ego consciousness.

In addition to *being fear-based, reactionary-based, and conflict-based, ego-creating is also survival-based*. The ego consciousness was very useful during the early stages of human evolution. Since the primary motive was survival, and the basic fear response in the face of danger was flight or fight, ego consciousness contributed to our survival.

One of the interesting questions I like to ask people is, "What is your purpose in life?" This question makes them think about life and about what is important to them, and it

Ego-creating Phases

usually reveals whether or not they are at the level of ego-creating or the level of LoveAge-creating.

When I asked a man this question, I can remember him saying, "To survive." He was literally in an ego survival mode concerning his finances, home foreclosure, social relationships, health, and life in general. Another man told me that his life purpose was, "To work my butt off and die."

A woman said to me that her purpose was, "to procreate." This was another form of survival, which involved passing on her genes for the survival of her biological self. These answers were indications that the people were most likely living in the me-creating phases, where some form of survival was paramount. Next to fear, survival is one of the ego's primary motivation.

Today, fear and other ego reactions contribute to a dysfunctional world where conflict-riddled relationships, combined with world-destroying technologies, threaten the possible extinction of the human species. Secular or materialistic approaches to ego-creating operate without concern for the Divine or for God's input. The "me" victimized by life's circumstances is the creator that relies on irrational emotional responses or habits and sometimes on rational/scientific solutions. There is often a belief that technology will solve problems and will be the salvation of humanity. So who needs the Divine?

When me-creating includes God, that God is usually wrathful. A polarization of "me vs. God" also exists, where "me" tries to appease or gain God's favor in order to get what's best for me. A wrathful God is a random force that places the "me" in a victim role. The relationship with God is usually a father/child arrangement where God is the overbearing parent and the source of wrath when the child does not obey. But wrath can happen even when the "child" seems to be obeying.

The ego level of consciousness views relationships as being separate, polarizing, conflicting, and victimizing. The "me vs. others" is a conflict over scarce resources, which become the major source of greed, wars, inequality, starvation, and a lot of unhappiness and grief. *Ego-creating is me-based, polarized-based, and victim-based.*

Another common attribute of ego-creating is to think that creating should happen by manipulating things outside oneself. The "me" tries to manipulate the external environment to create better circumstances or material things or to change others for the "me's" benefit. Ego-creating processes change from the outside to the inside. It's *outside/inside-based* creating. Those engaged in ego-creating think that what's outside in the physical, social, and spiritual environments is what causes their inner circumstances of unhappiness. The cause of difficulties lies without rather than within themselves and external circumstances or others is what needs to be changed.

The ego consequently avoids being responsible at all costs when trying to solve problems or trying to create a better situation. *Ego-creating is irresponsible-based.* Since the causes of life's difficulties are outside oneself, the ego is always defending itself against other's attacks and trying to change others, who are viewed as being wrong or the problem.

Ego-creating is mostly an unconscious or at best a semi-conscious activity. Generally, there is an unconscious reaction to external difficulties that ignite the ego habits stored within the subconscious mind. *Ego-creating is unconscious-based.*

Ego-creating Phases

The ego consciousness also has basic ways it empowers or creates life. Some use the victim role to control others or their circumstances. They may also try to manipulate the random forces of chance, luck, or God's wrath. Some use controlling others through complaints, anger, greed, mental willpower, or even violence to obtain selfish desires. Others, especially the academicians, use the rational mind to devise rational models for making decisions. For example, economic rational models tried to predict irrational economic behavior during the decade before the great recession of 2008 and failed miserably. To predict economic models based on the ego consciousness they need to be based on extreme greed.

Me-creating

The basic motivating force of me-creating involves getting what is good-for-me in order to make sure that the ego survives and gets what it wants. Figure 10.1 is an illustration of the me-creating phase that you might be experiencing or may already have transitioned from. It shows the creative-three elements, which are the *me, other,* and the *Divine.* The "me" in this phase receives the overwhelming benefit of what's created.

The "me" can also be the victim of the difficulties created in the social environment as well as by God's wrath. The representations of God or the Divine in this illustration and all others indicate how humans perceive God rather than indicating the actual appearance or nature of God. Also, God is not human looking, so the human illustration, at best, is a poor substitute image of the Divine.

If this were an illustration for believers in the secular/materialist world view, there would be no representation of a wrathful God. The creative process in a dualistic model of society would only exist between "me" and "others," and luck or chance would be viewed as the wrath of the universe.

Me-creating is the main mode by which most people relate to others in order to create their environments. For the first four decades of my life, I viewed luck as the primary determinant in much the same way as my grandmother did. It seemed as though I was in a conflict with the universe to minimize bad luck. To avoid bad luck, I practiced some superstitions such as hanging a rabbit's foot on my belt loop, not opening umbrellas in the house, or not walking under a ladder. However, I didn't take it to the extent of doing the kinds of things my grandmother did for bingo luck.

I sort of resigned myself to the universe's luck and felt little or no responsibility for creating life's destiny. Luck and God's wrath disempowered me. I was at the mercy of the unpredictable winds of luck and wrath that blew me around like a leaf into unwanted circumstances and consequences.

If You Think Life's Created by Luck and Chance, You'll Live in a Powerless Trance

God's Wrath and My Victim Consciousness

As a teenage member of the Methodist Church, I learned the importance of fearing God's wrath as another of those uncertain universal forces. God's wrath was similar to bad luck since it came at unexpected times and I wasn't sure

Ego-creating Phases

Figure 10.1

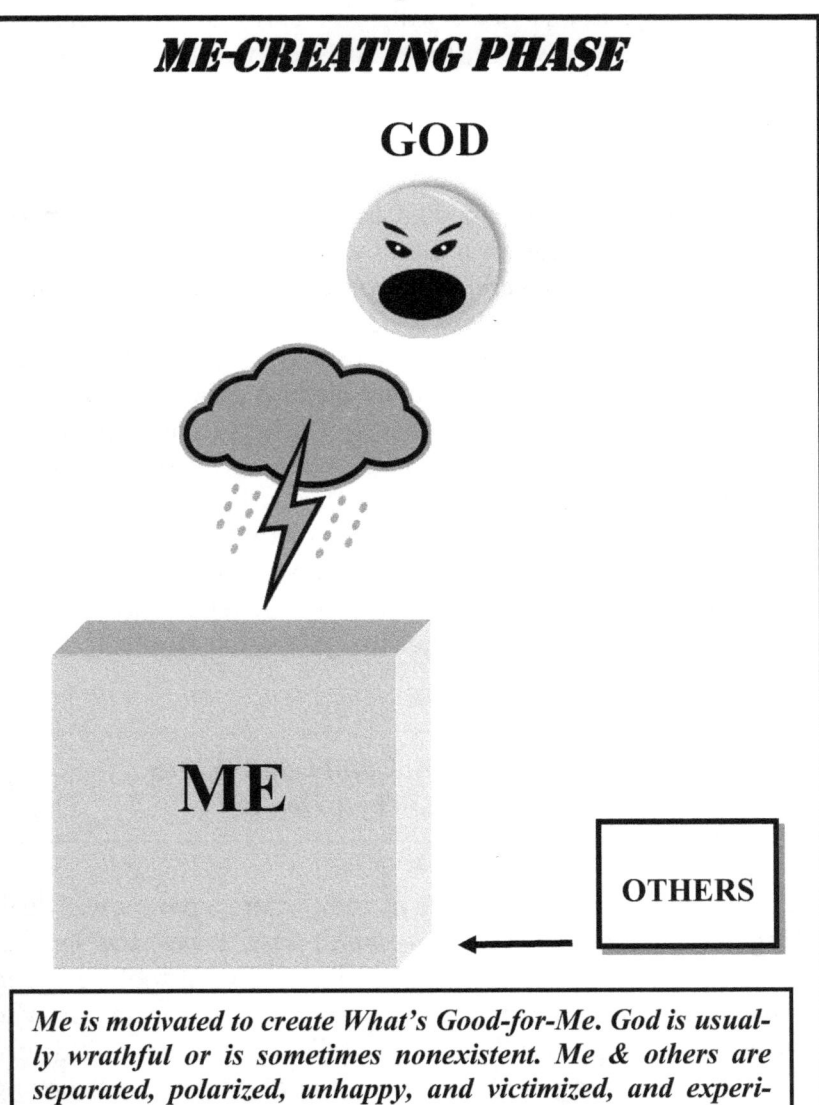

ME-CREATING PHASE

Me is motivated to create What's Good-for-Me. God is usually wrathful or is sometimes nonexistent. Me & others are separated, polarized, unhappy, and victimized, and experience conflict over scarce resources for survival.

why I was experiencing it. I also learned that when something went wrong, it was God's will, which was a softer version of God's wrath. As a youth, I viewed God's wrath and/or luck as the basic forces creating my destiny.

***

When my cousin died as a child, I learned from the church that her death was God's will. I wondered why God did such mean things to children, and I feared that God might do them to me someday. Now, I view children's deaths usually as part of a spiritual plan that they usually established with their parents on the inner plane before birth. A child's death usually serves as a gift that allows parents or others to learn lessons or to gain spiritual understanding. When my cousin died, her parents turned to religion, and as far as I could tell, it made advancements in their spiritual understanding. One of her sisters made a great deal of spiritual advancement, but I'm not sure how much of it was related to her sister's death. As I see it, my cousin's death was a spiritual gift to her family.

Most Believe Luck and God's Wrath Determine Their Destiny

In another experience in 2010, where a parent was dealing with a death of a young adult son, I saw the lack of understanding of this gift and saw how a parent took refuge in the victim consciousness. The parent was a contractor who was remodeling my home, and we talked about his son's death. He was swimming in the victimization of grief and was having a difficult time keeping his business afloat. He was fortunate that one of his workers kept it operating.

Ego-creating Phases

We all have a choice of accepting the gift of a child's death, of disability, or of any other difficulty for our spiritual maturity. This may sound cruel, but it was most likely something the child's and parents' Souls agreed to on the inner plane before the child's birth. In families, we are truly co-planners helping each other experience lessons for the unfoldment of the spiritual consciousness of love. This is why family members tend to keep reincarnating over and over in the same extended family. Those under ego's victim consciousness have a very difficult time accepting these difficulties as gifts for learning.

Have you ever had to make a choice about how to handle a family or a friend's death or some other kind of loss?

Using Victim Forces to Control Others

During the me-creating phase of my life, I felt that I had some power by controlling others. One way I controlled others as mentioned earlier was to make others feel sorry for me as a "poor victim" of the universe. If they felt sorry for me, they would do something to help me. I became aware of this ego habit when I was in college, but it took me years to minimize the use of it.

Complaining was a more powerful force for controlling others. I judged and blamed others for their inappropriate behavior in order to control them and get what I wanted. I was also protecting my ego since things that happened in my life were never viewed as my fault or responsibility. My problems stemmed from the faults of others or from some outside forces that victimized me.

Your Creative Power of Love

The ego lives in conflict in order to empower and protect itself as well as to control others. In order to do this, my primary way of empowerment was mainly to use emotional and mental forces. Some of the other emotional tactics used for manipulating others were anger, jealousy, gossip, fears, lies, shame, criticism, guilt, diminishment of another's self-worth, threats, prejudice, and intolerance, to name a few.

As a college student, I learned that God's wrath and luck were not the only external factors affecting me. When I studied sociology, I began to wonder how much my life had been determined by my parents' socialization, by society's uncaring and ego-dominated institutions, by culture, or by poor genetic inheritance. These factors became additional external forces contributing to my disempowerment.

The masses of humanity are in a victim state of disempowerment, as I was for about the first 40 years or more of life. The ego consciousness lives in a state of disempowerment when it comes to self-directing or co-directing life. Also, oppressive governments, parents, cultures, political ideologies, religious dogma and rituals, commercial ads, and other social controls contribute to the victim state of consciousness. LoveAge-creators do not let people or institutions with military boots march through their minds and emotions. Control your own life with the loving assistance of the Divine.

Beware of Military Boots Marching Through Your Mind

What are the different kinds of ego controls from society and family that march through your mind?

Ego-creating Phases

Power of an Empty Feeling

In addition to eventually realizing that difficulties were lessons for me to learn from, I was helped in other ways by the Divine during the me-creating phase. My parents never attended church when I was a child, but they were good, moral people. When I became a teenager, I had an inner feeling of emptiness about my parents' life. As I look back on this experience, it must have been Soul's dissatisfaction prompting me to search for a solution. My inner feeling of emptiness pushed me to learn higher forms of love. This emptiness was a power that motivated me toward love, spirituality, and higher forms of creating, but I was not aware of what was happening to me at the time I felt emptiness within. Fortunately, it helped motivate me to do things to grow spiritually.

Roger Walsh, in his book, *Essential Spirituality*, referred to this emptiness as "divine discontent." This uneasy inner feeling of emptiness served to push me up higher rungs of my destiny's spiritual ladder. I didn't realize it at the time, but this divine uneasiness was a source of inner guidance and wisdom telling me that it was time to move on to something else. Fortunately, this empowerment tool was available during the time I was under the control of the ego consciousness.

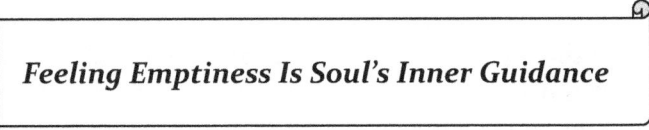

Feeling Emptiness Is Soul's Inner Guidance

Have you ever felt divine discontent or a sense of emptiness pushing you forward spiritually?

Another source of guidance available to me during the me-creating phase was the mental awareness of how pain created by my ego habits caused me to seek solutions. Eventually, I realized that the good-for-me motivation did not create the harmony and happiness in relationships that I desired. The turning point for this stage occurred when I was in college and decided to open my heart to others' good through social religion and nonviolent change.

Other-creating

For some, the me-creating consciousness moves into other-creating when the main motive is to do what is good-for-others. This phase is based on sacrificial love, where one tries to maximize others' good at the expense of "me." This is where social justice, equality, world peace, feeding and healing the poor, saving animals or the environment become important.

Evolution of Sacrifice

In most early religions, sacrifice was a relationship that existed between God and humans for thousands and thousands of years. Humans thought they had to sacrifice something to God to appease Him, to show fear of Him, to stop His wrath, or to make God beholden for returning favors.

In the biblical story of Abraham, he was about to thrust a knife into his son, Isaac, who was bound and lying on an altar. An angel appeared, telling him that he had passed the test of fearing God and that he didn't have to sacrifice his son. Abraham saw a ram nearby, and he decided that animals were more appropriate as a sacrifice than humans. This marked the transition in Judaism to sacrificing animals instead of humans.

Ego-creating Phases

I watched a documentary on TV about Peruvians sacrificing children to their gods of the oceans, the mountains, and the sun. These types of sacrifices were also practiced throughout other parts of the world.

Sometime between 600 and 200 BC, the practice of sacrificing took a turn toward a God desiring compassion rather than the sacrifice of humans or animals. Spiritual giants taught about the God of compassion rather than a wrathful God, but this belief did not take hold in the cultures of that time. Today, we may be completing this task of realizing a compassionate God if the Love Age materializes.

Unfortunately, the concept of sacrifice has not been eliminated from religions, even in today's world. Antiabortion violence is a form of self-sacrificing used by those against abortion whom some authorities refer to as "Christian terrorists." In the United States, it is estimated that to date there have been eight abortion providers killed (four doctors, two clinic employees, a security guard, and a clinic escort), all in the name of religious dogma. In such cases, if the "Christian terrorists" were caught, they believed they sacrificed their lives for a prison or worse sentence. They believe in a form of self-sacrificing for other's good.

The actions of terrorists who fly planes into buildings or who strap bombs on to sacrifice themselves and those they are against are similar to actions performed according to earlier religious sacrificial practices, except that in these cases, the actions involve self-sacrifice. But these acts are still modern day interpretations of the concept of sacrificing to appease God. These people believe their actions are a form of sacrificing for the good-of-others or 27 virgins.

Your Creative Power of Love

***

Have you heard about the terrorist bomber who arrived at the gates of heaven after blowing up himself and many others? He asked the gatekeeper, "Where are my 27 virgins?"

"Oh, you must have misunderstood. It wasn't 27 virgins; it was 27 Virginians. You have something very important to learn from them. Haven't you heard that their state slogan is, *'Virginia Is for Lovers'*?"

Even if the terrorist had received 27 virgins, it would seem to be a high price to pay for less than a month's worth of virgins. Men sometimes do stupid things because of their libido. I have often wondered what the women who strap on bombs are promised. Since their cultures are usually male dominated, I would think that they would hold out for something more than virgins. Twenty-seven male slaves for eternity might seem to be a better deal. What do you think?

***

Mother Teresa was a modern example of self-sacrificing for the good-of-others. She lived a life of poverty in order to serve the poor. After her death, I read the article, "Mother Teresa's Crisis of Faith" in *Time* magazine, August 23, 2007. The article was about her life and her desire for a direct spiritual relationship with Jesus and God. She had written to Rev. Michael Van Der Peet for religious counseling in September of 1979, and the following is her statement. "Jesus has a very special love for you. As for me, the silence and the emptiness is so great that I look and do not see, listen and do not hear."

Ego-creating Phases

Figure 10.2

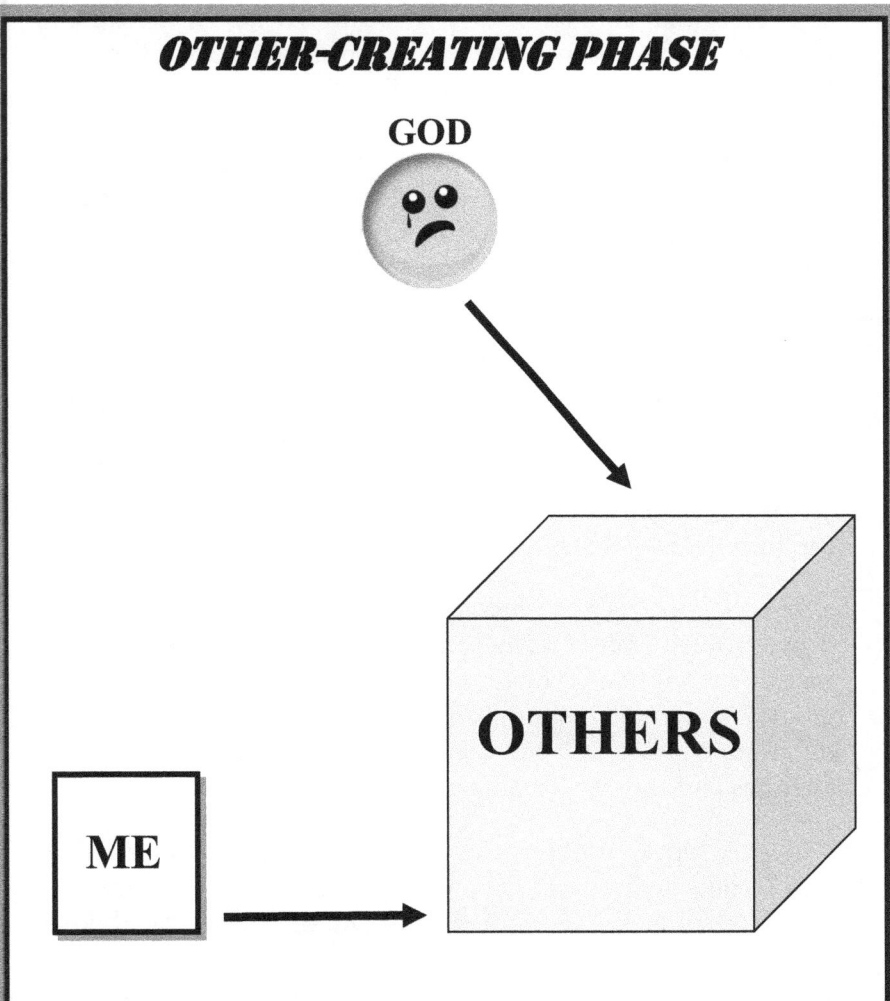

Your Creative Power of Love

She was deeply bothered that she could not establish a direct spiritual contact of love with the Divine. At the time of the article, the Catholic Church was in the process of making her a saint for her life of self-sacrifice. She chose the dogma of the church rather than what her own heart desired for a meaningful relationship with the Divine. Self-sacrificing was a step in her spirituality, but it never met her deep yearning for spiritually experiencing Jesus or God like the experiences she had earlier in her life.

Fortunately, there are many, many more today who sacrifice themselves peacefully for the good-of-others. They believe that their sacrificing for the good-of-others and doing good works is what God wants for their life. This is a much higher type of sacrificial love than the practice of sacrificing children, other humans, or animal life or of sacrificing one's self in order to kill others.

Sacrificing has tended to evolve out of sacrificing children, women, and conquered prisoners to the stage of the sacrifice of animals. Today, sacrificing that is based on a religious justification seems primarily to have evolved into two different types of self-sacrificing—self-sacrificing to kill one's enemies and self-sacrificing to help others.

A representation of other-creating is found in Figure 10.2. Others rather than the "me" become the main beneficiaries of what is to be created. Instead of self-centered love, sacrificial love becomes the motivation. It is a step toward greater love if it does not include killing others, which also helps advance the vibrations of love for the collective good. Its problem is that it does not include what is good for the "me" or the Divine's desire for the good of the whole.

Ego-creating Phases

What is Other-creating?

In the other-creating phase, God is usually viewed as a sacrificing and/or compassionate source of creation and the "me" needs to emulate the same form of sacrificial love on Earth. The "me" is to sacrifice itself for others' good. This was the main type of love I learned as a teenager in church. Even Jesus was sacrificed for my sins.

See Figure 10.2 for an illustration of how the creative threes of me, others, and God relate to each other in other-creating. The three elements are still viewed as separate, but they have a different motivation. This time, the motivation is to create for the good-of others. Sacrificing became paramount rather than survival. God is the God of compassion, and humans should be compassionate and sacrifice for the good-of-others.

The choice that helped me transition into the other-creative state of consciousness derived from my college experiences. It broadened my mind's perspective beyond what I knew and believed in as a fundamentalist Christianity. As I look back on the decision to attend college, it too was set up by outside forces.

In an earlier chapter, I told this story about roadblocks that had the Divine Spirit's fingerprints all over them. Sometimes, the Divine pushed me into situations by setting up circumstances that shoved me one way or the other. When the coal mines laid off miners, the layoff contributed to my spiritual destiny by blocking my option of being a miner, leading me instead to consider the possibility of a college education. This was another way the Divine helped guide me early in life when I was still in an unconscious ego state.

> ***Destiny Is Not Predestined; It's the Cumulative Result of the Divine's Guidance, Karma, and Your Choices***

My mind as a source of creating was a double-edged sword. On one side, it created my ego consciousness and hardened habits that were difficult to change. But on the other edge were the mental abilities for analyzing, recognizing the problems of ego's habits, and realizing the habits that needed changing. My college education started to bring out the powers of the mind to allow me to initiate changes in my life and to open me to alternative solutions.

Social Empowerment in Religion and Science

At West Virginia Wesleyan College, I transitioned into the other-creating consciousness and made a shift from faith-based religion to social religion and evidence-based science. The driving force behind these changes related to choosing a liberal interpretation of the Bible, selecting sociology as a major, and wanting to live a nonviolent life. I was shifting from faith-based to evidence-based knowing, and I wanted to change the world to a more peaceful and just place to live. This was when I ignited the good-for-others or the sacrificial love phase of creating.

These choices moved the other-creating phase into high gear, where I believed the powers of nonviolence and the knowledge of sociology could help create a better social environment here on Earth. This spiritual goal became more important than the desire for salvation and going to heaven, which had previously been a good-for-me survival motivation for the afterlife. I was now moving into the consciousness of what's good-for-others, which was a higher phase of love.

Ego-creating Phases

Chose liberal Christianity. I shared in an earlier chapter an experience of the New Testament Bible class at West Virginia Wesleyan College, in which I moved from a fundamentalist interpretation of the Bible to a liberal one, which was based on evidence. This was a significant choice that helped me move from a faith-based to an observational or evidence-based consciousness.

I was beginning to rely on the importance of observations instead of having a faith-based reliance on religious dogma, secondhand knowledge, and myths. This helped open my mind to a focus on changing the social environment as well as on creating more social justice and world peace. This was a turning point that opened my heart to help others.

Chose Nonviolence. I briefly mentioned some of the following experiences in an earlier chapter, and I will expand on them in order to shed more light on my ego-creating. I left the Methodist Church since I had a deep feeling of emptiness while attending worship services and even felt alienated from God when I attended them. During this time, I struggled with my blind faith in the Bible. I was also struggling with the question of how to relate to what was going on in the early 1960's, with the civil rights and peace movements. I was shifting my religious consciousness toward social religion where I became more concerned about establishing heavenly peace, justice, and love here on Earth.

After reading a book by Mahatma Gandhi, I was committed to a nonviolent life. Nonviolence was a moral and collective way to change society's institutions in order to make them more peaceful and just. I couldn't understand why the Methodist Church did not see the importance of Jesus's teaching about turning the other cheek. Nonviolence was an element of Jesus's teaching of love and of sacrificing oneself for others.

Jesus was also a social activist, and he supported those who were treated unjustly during his times. The synagogues and temples did not allow the sick, the poor, and the prostitutes to attend services. The religious leaders of the time hated Samaritans and treated them unfairly. Jesus taught tolerance and the love of everyone. Loving one another was his approach to life, even when the other person was an enemy. I wondered why the church wasn't teaching and doing more about today's injustices. Why weren't they more interested in world peace than in justifying wars?

My belief in nonviolence as a moral power grew, and I realized that it could help make groups into powerful agents for changing social institutions. This realization gave me an opportunity to take an active role with others in creation rather than standing back and letting God or luck do it. This activity was a source of social empowerment, and I was becoming more conscious of the importance of joining with others to use nonviolence as a source of empowerment.

> *Other-creating Can be Used as a Collective Empowerment to Change Social Institutions*

Sociology and social change. At the same time that I was going through this transition in religious consciousness, I was in the process of deciding what my college major would be. I decided on sociology, which was another choice for evidence-based knowing by means of the scientific method.

Ego-creating Phases

When I studied sociology at West Virginia Wesleyan College, I believed it would lead to a more reliable source of information about social behavior and about how to do peaceful social change. Since sociology used firsthand observations and scientific methodologies, it was evidence-based and used research to control scientists' personal biases to capture the actual reality of observed social behavior. In addition, other scientists could duplicate the research to recheck the reality of a study's conclusions. Scientific methods used rigorous means to check the validity of data.

I wanted to use sociology to further my scientific understanding of social change as well as to further nonviolence in order to make a better world. I hoped to combine these two to create a world where social and racial justice as well as world peace would thrive. I even pursued a doctor's degree in the field of sociology at the University of Pittsburgh with this motivation in mind.

As much as possible, I wanted my beliefs to be based on objective evidence and verifiable experiences. I didn't want faith to be my final validation for what I believed. I saw faith as a starting point rather than as an end for knowing until I could find more objective or experiential source of information to support or not support what I believed.

Later in life, I eventually understood another aspect of the faith that Jesus taught. Rather than using it to believe in church dogma or beliefs, faith was a way for me to move mountains to change myself or the world as well as for healing myself. Unfortunately, at that time, I felt that I only had the power to move tiny molehills and that I wasn't worthy to be healed.

Your Creative Power of Love

Nonviolence and sociology gave me a belief in the power of other-creating. I felt that I was taking steps toward understanding the world more objectively and that would help make it more peaceful. However, I became no more than a nonviolent theorist or idealist rather than a nonviolent activist.

Even though I believed in the possibility of changing social life, sociology caught me in another web, in which I realized that there were additional social factors controlling my own life. It helped expand my victim state of consciousness, to an extent. Sociology was like a double-edged sword, which gave me the hope of understanding social change. At the same time, it made me realize that the social environment, especially in the form of institutions, was the primary cause of my ego beliefs and behaviors.

Emptiness of Quakers and nonviolence. I joined a Quaker meeting in Salem, Ohio, after graduating from West Virginian Wesleyan College and accepting an English and social studies teaching position at the Leetonia High School. Since Quakers believed in nonviolence, I became a member of this group in order to associate with like-minded believers. I was not much of an activist, and I did not get involved in nonviolent protests, but my heart supported the peace movement both during the Vietnam War and during the racial and social justice changes of the 1960s and 1970s. I believed that my primary role was to understand violence, nonviolence, and social change from a scientific perspective in order to contribute information to help create a more peaceful and just world.

I was impressed with the earlier Quaker leaders such as George Fox, who used the experiences of the "Inner Light" or the "Christ within" to find inner peace. Their beliefs and practices about nonviolence evolved from the peace and love they

Ego-creating Phases

found within. The Quakers started out as a mystical Christian group.

***

At the first Quaker meeting I attended, one of the members asked me, "How did you find out about Quakers?"

"I read about George Fox and the early Quakers in college since I was interested in nonviolence. I was very impressed with their ability to experience the 'Inner Light,' which was where their inner peace derived from."

"Well, we're not like that anymore..."

I didn't fully understand his response, but after a while, I realized that seeking the guidance of the "Inner Light" or of the "still, small voice of God" within to find a deep sense of inner peace was no longer practiced by most Quakers. A Quaker in Pittsburgh told me that the meetings there were more like academic popcorn machines, in which one Quaker gave a rational talk followed by others popping up to give their academic or rational responses or rebuttals. The Pittsburgh Quaker meeting relied on reasoning and on the mind rather than on inner spiritual experiences of peace.

I became disillusioned with the Quakers and with nonviolence as a way to change the world. However, I'm not suggesting that society cannot be changed by nonviolent methods, since Mahatma Gandhi's and Martin Luther King's nonviolent methods are proof that it can be done.

> ### *Nonviolence is a Moral Means of Other-creating*

When I joined the Quakers, I desired nonviolence, but when I left the Quakers, I was more interested in experiencing the "Inner Light" or the "still, small voice of God" and the inner peace it brought. This interest started my search for establishing a direct relationship with the Divine rather than following the outer religious dogmas and secondhand experiences handed down by churches.

The main consciousness change during the other-creating phase was that I widened my heart to find ways to help others solve the world's social problems. This is the same kind of movement that is happening in Christianity today. The book by Rick Warren, *The Purpose Driven Life*, along with his worldwide programs to help with hunger, health, and other problems, are examples of other-creating in action.

Some who go through this stage do not get involved in a religious organization but instead join all types of humanitarian, environmental, and animal rights programs in order to try to make the world a better place to live for all life. As I went through this stage, it helped broaden my heart to focus on others' needs.

Emptiness of Sociology

When I was teaching at Westminster College in the mid-1970s and was still working on my PhD, I started to feel an inner emptiness and disillusionment with sociology and its possible contributions to nonviolence and the creation of a better world. I expected the social sciences to contribute to the

Ego-creating Phases

understanding of nonviolent change and world peace, but the light they shed on these problems was akin to the light that came from a flashlight with dead batteries. Sociology and most of the other human sciences focused on the ego, while my spiritual experiences were telling me that the ego was the primary cause of the world's problems.

I became disillusioned with sociology, and my heart was no longer interested in teaching it. I eventually decided to stop working on my PhD at the University of Pittsburgh. But since this work was a condition for continued employment at Westminster College and for receiving tenure, I knew that this decision meant I would have to leave college teaching. My ego search for personal happiness in a career was evaporating in a lack of purpose and motivation to be a sociologist.

In the late 1970s, I didn't know what career would satisfy my emptiness; this period was a confusing, difficult time. When I tried being a carpenter and then tried being a marriage, family, and child counselor, I experienced emptiness again. The pushing force of spirit moved me toward other options. Finally, I chose to be a computer system analyst, and my empty feeling about a career was relatively satisfied until I decided to retire at 59 in order to write this book.

I was also embroiled in other turmoil. Who was I, and what was the meaning of life? This was the period right before the turning point of the "Amanda Dream" experience. With all this turmoil in my life, I was beginning to move away from the other-creating phase, to look for other answers.

Have you ever thought you had found a way to make the world a better place to live and later became disillusioned with it?

Your Creative Power of Love

Push and Pull Forces Affecting Destiny

Did you notice that during the me-creating and other-creating phases of my life, the primary force pushing me in different directions was the Divine using my *karma to* set up situations where I had to make choices? Later, I learned that I was responsible and earned my circumstances and my lessons of love. I was personally responsible for my circumstances since I was the one who had created the *karma* in this life or in past lives.

Going through these circumstances was the main way of nudging my unconscious ego "me" into situations that would help me learn needed lessons. Inner feelings of emptiness or uneasiness, circumstances blocking my desires, and new opportunities opening up had pushed me away from old, worn-out religious paths, careers, or other belief systems that tried to teach me how to create my life.

The feelings of emptiness tended to happen before major changes in my life, and they served as difficulties, new opportunities, and feelings of despair that motivated me to move forward. However, I was always the one who had to make the final decision about the forces pushing me around. Pulling forces, such as conscious intentions that could be used to direct my life, were not in my tool bag of creative tools earlier in life, but they became more important in later phases of creating.

I'm not suggesting that you have to go through either of the phases of ego-creating. You might have started at a higher level of love or started at other-creating. You might also have started with me-creating and skipped over other-creating to reach higher levels of creating with love.

Ego-creating Phases

Do not think that you have to live the journey of creating life the way my life unfolded. We all have freedom of choice and different situations to learn from, and this fact makes the creating path a unique experience for all. You should also know that progressing from the self-centered love of the me-creating stage to the self-sacrificing love of other-creating does increase the energy vibrations of love within yourself as well as in the world. Congratulations on any improvement you made in raising your vibrations of love!

The next chapter will look at the transitions I went through in order to move on to higher levels of creating with love. These transitions helped me move from ego-creating to LoveAge-creating.

Figure 10.3

SUGGESTED QUESTIONS FOR PERSONAL AND GROUP DISCUSSION

1. Are you aware of a spiritual plan for your life?
2. Are you operating in the me-creating or other-creating phase?
3. Have you ever felt you were a victim of chance, luck, or God's wrath?
4. Are you using mental and emotional ego habits to control others?
5. Have you ever had a feeling of emptiness about life that helped push you forward in your spiritual growth?
6. Have you ever experienced a death or difficulty in life that you now see as a gift for spiritual growth?
7. Do you let people march through your mind and emotions with military boots?

Chapter Eleven

Transitional Phase

The transitional phase between ego-creating and LoveAge-creating includes two major realizations—ego-realization and soul-realization. In my life, they were phases which had long learning periods and overlapped each other, and had fuzzy boundaries between them. Please remember these phases are mental constructions that helped me understand what went on in my life while I was learning to create my life with love. Your experiences may be much different, but I'm sure there will be some similarities.

Most of my learning about ego-realization occurred somewhere between 1960 and the 1990s. This learning was a slow, painful process, during which upsurges occurred in recognizing my ego responses and habits, after which there were long periods of stagnation.

The soul-realization phase probably started in the mid-1970s, and I'm still experiencing it today. Soul-realization moved me away from mental observations by the ego and toward the Soul observing my ego habits from a wiser, more encompassing and compassionate perspective. Soul also had more power to control ego reactions by recognizing them at the time of their initial reactions.

As I look back over the places where my journey of learning to be a Love Age creator has taken me, I've wondered how I moved from ego-creating to being able to empower myself with love. These stages tended to follow a progression of experiences, but you may have a different progression of stages or may possibly already have started LoveAge-creating.

I do not know much about Eckhart Tolle's life, but he seemed to have shifted his consciousness from the ego-creating phases to oneness-creating in one night. This is what is known as a revolutionary change since it happened so fast.

During the first two years after his experience, he lived on a park bench, probably interpreting what his spiritual experiences meant as well as learning how to balance them and his new empowerment with the experience of living in the physical and social worlds. It is very unusual to progress as quickly as Eckhart Tolle did, and most of you, as I did, will probably mature spiritually at a slower pace by taking smaller steps. The difference between Tolle and me was the letter "R." My change was evolutionary while his was "r-evolutionary."

Fortunately, there are signs that the pace of spiritual empowerment is increasing, since the collective consciousness has heightened its vibrations. This will help all of us to become Love Age creators at a quicker pace.

As a realized Divine Self, you are already spiritually evolved or at the top of your creative abilities. You just have to realize that you are already Soul, a powerful creator of love. Soul is already at the peak of spirituality and empowerment, and the purpose of your journey is to learn to realize it.

Figure 11.1

TRANSITIONAL PHASES

SOUL-REALIZED

Recognize True Self as Soul

EGO-REALIZED

Mental Recognition of Ego Habits

> *Empowerment Journeys Are Usually
> Small Steps rather than One Big Leap*

Ego-realization Phase

When I started to become ego-realized, it was the turning point that initiated the end of the ego-creating phases. I mentally became aware of how ego habits controlled me and contributed to life's difficulties and pain. I cannot pinpoint a time when this first happened, but it might have occurred at the time when I recognized how I used the "poor me" victim habit during my college student days.

Ego-realization was a long, drawn-out process. Clearly recognizing the habits or other circumstances that created difficulties or unhappiness is the first step in changing any kind of behavior in life.

> *Change Starts with Recognizing Ego's Habits*

Early in the 1970s, I found myself working on controlling the wide emotional swings of anger, distrust, and other unproductive ego reactions. It wasn't until the early 1990s when I recognized my most serious ego habit of complaining and decided to do something about it.

I discussed in a previous chapter how my wife and I became aware of our complaining/guilt relationship and how we tried to solve it with the mind. We tried unsuccessfully to tell each other when we noticed the other using guilt or complaints. The mental solution at times did more to stir up more ego reactions than to stop the disharmony. When I eventually recognized the deeper levels of fear that underlie my ego reactions, I gained a deeper understanding of the workings of the ego.

It's futile to try to correct another's ego problems since the attempt will most likely ignite an ego war. Since you can only change yourself, just focus on replacing your own ego habits with spiritual ones or with love. Be an example of love, and forget about changing others. Be patient; most Love Age pioneers evolve over time by replacing one ego habit at a time. This gradual process will most likely be the predominant way of change during the Love Age.

What is the most prevalent way in which your ego brings conflicts and unhappiness into your life?

To a degree, the mind can control emotions. Back in the 1970s, I began to gain some control over the broad swings of my emotions. Ego-realization starts with the mind recognizing its unproductive reactions and habits and then, to an extent, controlling them through mental observations.

But an ego-realized person understands that the ego mind and its habits are detrimental to peace, happiness, and love. When one also realizes that the world of the human ego and of matter is built on nothing more than mental illusions, ego-realization takes another step toward LoveAge-creating.

In my life, the ego-realization phase primarily involved recognition of my ego habits and how fear ignited their unconscious emotional reactions to create a life of conflict and pain. The mind's power of analysis and observation helped me start to control my emotional responses, but I gradually realized that there was a limit to the mind's control over ego's reactions.

I started to transition from the ego-realization phase when I had an awareness of most of my ego habits and their related fears. The nail in the coffin occurred at a higher level of spiritual realization when I gained a degree of soul awareness that could recognize, control, and stop what happened at the ego's initial point of reaction to difficulties. For a while, I felt straddled between the world of the ego and spirit, but this eased off when I transitioned into the phase of soul-realization.

Are you ego-realized???

I viewed the ego and the mind, the primary sources of empowerment during the ego-creating phases, as being too limited to carry me any further along my journey of love empowerment. I had to make a major shift from the mental and social sources of power to a consciousness where intentions, inner guidance, and love became the sources of power. This was the point where being soul-realized really started to change the ego as soul's tool box of power became available.

Shifting from Ego-realization to Soul-realization

In the ego state of consciousness, humans are unconscious operators, and as they make the transition between the human and spirit worlds, they become semi-conscious and eventually live in full soul consciousness. The mind and its socially constructed illusions are in control before the transition into soul-realization, but as Soul increases in power, it eventually controls the mind, emotions, and imagination. These are the important tools for creating your life. As you become a more realized being, you serve as a clearer channel for the Divine's love and wisdom, and you know your part in the Divine's plan.

The infrequent experiences I initially had of the spiritual consciousness made me feel trapped in the unwanted human consciousness of the ego. Physical eyes cannot see into the spiritual worlds. At times, I felt like I was in sort of a no-man's-land. But as I progressed in spiritual understanding and experiences, I began to feel more and more a part of the spiritual worlds. My spiritual eyes of Soul observed life from a higher perspective, in contrast to how ego's eyes looked up from the gutters of the material world.

Transitional Phase

Exactly when I transitioned from one phase to another was not clear. Sometimes aspects of soul-realization were mentally realized while operating in the ego consciousness. I believed mentally that I was Soul long before I could operate to some degree as a soul-realized being.

The same process occurred with love. When I had the "Amanda Dream," I gained a mental understanding of divine love, but I did not experience it from within until later in life. Most often, the phases started as a mental understanding, and over time, they slowly became a conscious experience of Soul and a way of life.

Psychics and Edgar Cayce

In 1969 or 1970, Audrey became a truth seeker when she had an inner experience of feeling the love of the Divine. I mentioned this experience earlier. She expanded the range of the types of books she read to include psychics who predicted things about the future as well as other spiritual subjects.

I was a professor at Westminster College during that time. I was mainly rooted in the academic ego consciousness. My commitment to scientific reasoning would not allow me to accept someone predicting the future. This sort of prediction just didn't appear to be scientifically possible. Eventually, after being shown examples of psychics who indeed predicted the future, I found that my hardened attachments to old beliefs about sources of useful knowledge cracking.

Audrey became interested in Edgar Cayce. After hearing how he could receive information while in trances that allowed him to heal people, I began to realize that valid information could be obtained from other sources than science. Divine wisdom from spiritual sources could be very useful.

Cayce also shared information about the death and rebirth process. I had already given up on the heaven and hell dogma that I was taught in church since no loving God would ever place one of his children in a state of hell for eternity. Maybe a wrathful God would but not a loving God. Even an ordinary earthly father who loved his child would not do that.

Ideas of reincarnation and *karma,* however, involved much more than just being shoved into hell for holding the wrong beliefs or doing the wrong actions. Cayce helped me believe that I had many lives in which to learn lessons resulting from the consequences of my ego's *karma.* This belief made me realize that life had purpose and that I wasn't living as a victim of luck or of God's wrath. I was the cause of my own circumstances and was responsible for changing them or for learning the needed lessons. This struck hard at my victim consciousness, and I knew that I had to be more responsible for creating my own destiny.

Have you experienced life as being purposeful?

Eckankar™

I had already left the Quakers because of a feeling of inner emptiness. I felt that they lacked a direct connection with the Divine's inner peace, which should have been their motivation for nonviolent beliefs and actions. After two or three years of reading about Edgar Cayce and after being in one of his book discussion groups in Hendersonville, North Carolina, Audrey and I felt we had received all we could from his teachings, and the feeling of spiritual emptiness arrived again. I was tired of hearing and reading about others who were having inner spiritual experiences. I wanted to have my own.

In 1971, a member of our Edgar Cayce study group received an announcement that Eckankar™ (known before 1985 as "The Ancient Science of Soul Travel") was going to have a discussion group in Ashville. Some of us decided to investigate what it and soul travel were all about. After reading one book and attending a meeting, Audrey and I decided to buy the discourses that allowed us to join the discussion group. At this point, we were both making a decision to move on with our spiritual life, and this time Audrey wasn't pulling me along. I felt that this new group might help me have those inner spiritual experiences that I had desired since being a Quaker.

Eckankar™ was a western adaptation of Shabda Yoga, an Eastern religion. It used contemplation as a means for one to project out of the body in order to experience inner spiritual worlds. But after years of practicing Eckankar contemplations, I still had never had an experience where I travelled and observed places or entities in the spiritual worlds. However, I did have experiences, mainly at seminars, where I would experience the inner light of God, a manifestation of Divine Energy. And much later, I came to experience the inner sound in meditation and eventually heard it while doing everyday activities.

At first, seeing the inner light and hearing the sound was an intermittent experience, and it took me some 25 years to establish a more frequent daily connection. The reason it took so long was that I had difficulty quieting and focusing the mind so I could experience the Divine's presence. Following the emphasis taught in Eckankar™, I had my goals set on projecting from the body rather than on experiencing the stillness and wisdom of the Divine.

During this time, I also used the mind to learn some of the self-help empowerment techniques for empowering life. I was introduced to setting goals, saying affirmations, and visualizing. These mental, emotional, and imaginative powers helped me direct my life. I learned to tap into the wisdom of the Divine with dreams, which I described early in the "Amanda Dream" experience.

I eventually realized that my mind did not have the power to understand what desires or actions were good-for-All. I realized more and more the limitations of the mind and the need to rely more on inner guidance and wisdom from the Divine. This realization also helped me understand that the material world and its ego illusions were becoming less important and that it was more important to connect with the spiritual worlds and its wisdom.

I realized that this stage of my spiritual development, where the power of the mind was primarily used, had to take a backseat. Understanding and experiencing the powers and wisdom of the inner spiritual worlds in order to help with my spiritual unfoldment and empowerment was much more important than what the limited mind had to offer. I also recognized that the power to choose my destiny increased as I spiritually matured.

Have you ever made a decision about a difficulty where the mind had serious limitations for helping you find a solution?

Soul-realization

I don't care who you are, one of the purposes for your current life is to realize your true identity as Soul. Soul-realization is the recognition and experiencing of yourself as the Divine Self and taking charge of the ego. You'll learn to use the tools Soul has for replacing the ego's habits with spiritual ones. Soul-realization also heightens the power of recognition, making it possible to catch ego reactions at the point when they occur. A realization and use of the power of the eight tools that Soul possesses will help you be a Love Age creator.

1. **Soul is the conscious observer.** Soul can consciously observe the thoughts, feelings, and circumstances of the inner mental and outer world as well as the divine dimensions. It is aware of what is unproductive in life and has the divine wisdom to know the best solutions.

   For example, I had to be aware of my ego complaining habit in order to know what I needed to change. Since Soul and not my own thought is *pure awareness*, it was the unit that consciously recognized ego's reactions. It also knew what the good-for-All solutions and actions were.

2. **Soul operates in the Now.** The ego operates in the past and future, while Soul operates in the now. The only time that you can do LoveAge-creating is in the present moment, since that is the only time and space in which the Divine exists and operates. The now is also the only time that we can experience the Divine as well as co-create with it. *LoveAge-creating only has now time where it can catch ego reacting at the time of a difficulty.*

3. **Soul operates by experiencing and being.** The ego is a doer or analyzer and operates by desiring (i.e., adding something) and fearing (i.e., worrying about losing something), while Soul uses experiencing and "being." You can only be what you have experienced and this is why I have continually shared my experiences and asked question throughout this book to get you to recognize your experiences and who you are as Soul.

    As Soul you are already all that you will ever be as a spiritual being, so just simply be what you already are. Soul creates changes in your life by just being what you ask or intend.

    I didn't want to be a complainer, and I had to learn to be divine love, to replace this ego habit. Conscious intentions evolve into the realization that you already are what you want, so just be that. All you have to do is just be divine love by thinking it, feeling it, imagining it, and doing it. This is being.

    A helpful technique for "being" is to use affirmations in the present tense. For example, I used the affirmation "I'm divine love or I'm love" to replace complaining attitudes and actions. This affirmation is more than just repeating the words. You should feel the love, see it in your imagination, think it, and do it when the opportunity occurs during the day.

Other affirmations I used were, "I'm filled with divine love," "I'm one with the still voice of the Divine," "I'm one with Soul, I feel its love, peace, and freedom, and I hear its stillness," and others. Since creative energy flows were the attention goes, being your affirmations will create the person you want to be.

You can also be divine love by going about your daily activities as though you are divine love in action. Creative action involves doing one thing at a time, with total attention to the quality and feeling of doing or being it. Divine love and complaining cannot exist at the same time and space, so one will replace the other depending on the focus of your awareness, attention, and actions. Being divine love replaces all ego habits.

4. **Soul is divine love.** Since Soul is of the essence of Divine Energy, which is divine love, the essence of Soul is also divine love. When Soul is in charge, divine love or the good-for-All intention flows through you to create divine love in your relationships and to solve difficulties. Your true self is love, so just be it.

5. **Soul consciously directs attention.** Consciousness is Divine Energy flowing from the Divine Source. Since Soul is the individualized essence of pure consciousness, it has the power to direct your attention consciously by means of focusing intentions. The power of consciousness is the power to focus attention, and this in turn affects the unmanifested energy, which attracts the things intended. When consciousness directs your thoughts, feelings, and imagination with intentions, it has the power to transform unmanifested energy from the Divine into manifested energy, forms, or situations.

Transitional Phase

***

Mikey had recently transferred into the second grade from another school. At recess, he was playing with his new friend, Tony. Mikey asked Tony, "I know where the American nation, German nation, and French nation are, but where is that Imagi-nation the teacher is always talking about?"

"I suppose it's anywhere you want it to be, Mikey."

"Huh?"

6. **Soul is the source of divine wisdom.** Divine Source, Divine Energy, and the Divine Self are your sources of divine wisdom for guiding spiritual intentions and actions. At the divine state of consciousness we learn through being, experiencing, and knowing. We do not know how we know something, but we just know it and this is how we can access divine wisdom for creating. When Soul is in charge and you access Divine Stillness, you have access to divine wisdom and to its guidance for creating what is good-for-All.

7. **Soul is one with the Divine.** Since Soul is made of Divine Energy, it is therefore divine too. You and every other person, no matter how much you are under the influence of the ego, are still divine beings. We are all made of the same Divine Energy that flows from the Divine Source and one with it as Soul. If you strike out to harm anyone, you strike out at the Divine in you too.

We need to be at least in a partnership with the Divine while still striving to be in a state of oneness with all life. The ego relationship of being separate or of having the father/child relationship with the Divine will not work. Soul lives in unity, while the ego exists as a separate state from others. Being one with the Divine, you also have the ability to live in harmony with the purpose and intentions of the Divine Source.

8. **Soul = Soul.** Since all Souls are Divine, we are all equal. Soul is not a member of a particular race, is male or female, old or young, smart or dumb, gay or straight, Christian or Buddhist, or any other characteristic that makes us different and separate in the ego world. Knowing that you are a Divine Self is knowing that you are equal to others and that they are equal to you. The gender bias toward male domination is changing, which originate from stories like Adam and Eve. Eve was the temptress and to blame for our evil ways, so past societies made females second class citizens. The female and male attributes need to be equalized rather than having one gender dominating another. As Soul there is no gender. The Divine uses Soul, regardless of gender, to help each other create life for the good-of-All.

> ***Humans Are Divine Beings Disguised in Ego Rags***

Soul-realization goes beyond being ego-realized in the process of becoming a wiser creator. It increases awareness, has power to focus attention, is peaceful and joyful, and has the capacity of divine love that places you in charge of the ego.

> ***Inner Peace & Joy Flow from Realizing Yourself as Soul***

It wasn't until soul awareness caught my mind complaining, at the time of the initial reaction of an ego habit, that I eventually gained real control. This happened some ten years after the ego-realization of my complaining habit. Soul eventually has to be in charge of both the mind and emotions and of their reactions in order to allow you to be a Love Age creator.

The reason for shifting from the ego self to the Divine Self is to take advantage of the tremendous amount of spiritual power that Soul has for consciously directing your destiny. Living with Soul in control leads to a personal transformation where you can live in harmony with the Divine's plan for peace, justice, security, abundance, joy, and love for all.

This way of living has become a necessity rather than an option, since humans are amassing technological powers that the conflicting ego consciousness may use to destroy us. Your decision to transform your identity and be Soul-realized is that important. I am not trying to frighten you with possible extinction but am just pointing out that it is one of the potential options of our future. We therefore need to take charge of our personal and collective destinies.

> *The More Soul Controls Thoughts and Feelings, the More You Control Your Destiny*

Soul Power Affects Collective Fields

The higher a person's energy vibrates with love, the greater his or her power will be. Some estimate that the top ten to fifteen percent of the population who have higher spiritual vibrations of love serve to balance out some of the negative ego energy of the rest of the world. Otherwise, the ego would already have destroyed us. Also, the higher your vibrations are, the greater the degree to which you will serve humanity by changing and heightening the consciousness of your own life and that of the communities you associate with.

Your Creative Power of Love

Are you willing to take one small step a day to increase your love vibrations for yourself and for the Love Age consciousness?

In groups, love increases in strength to a degree that is greater than the sum of its parts. This means that the sum of the energy vibrations of each person's love will be greater in a group than it is for that person as an individual. This collective power is a force that raises the power of people's ability to understand beyond their own personal spiritual consciousness, allowing the people in a group to have a greater impact on the world.

I have found that when I discuss spiritual books in a small group with others, it always helps me raise my ability to understand things beyond the level of my own personal consciousness. If the group has a negative consciousness, it will have a negative effect so be selective of the groups you join. In addition, a community of love helps raise the consciousness of the broader community's energy fields, and so on and so on.

While being in this stage of soul-realization, I learned to hear the outer or inner voice or the sounds of the spiritual dimensions. I knew Soul was pure energy and that it was a very powerful co-creator. I also began to realize the Divine's plan for myself and for the earth.

When I was in this stage, it took a long time for me to learn, to experience, and to trust the Divine. People like me who were immersed in the rational mind's consciousness have a difficult time struggling with the ego's mind, trusting the Divine, and letting go of mental attachments. Intellectual people have a difficult time being spiritual. But I feel that I am getting closer and closer to having Soul as the primary self and master of the ego.

The Divine Dwells Within Me as the True Me

Are you Soul-realized???

Soul-realization transferred me from following the parental leadership of ego empowerment to inwardly following my own Divine Self or Soul. We need to shift from playing follow-the-leader to following the Divine from within. Spirituality truly becomes an inner guidance system, like an inner GPS, flowing from my Divine Self.

In no way do I believe that I have completely learned or experienced everything I need to know about soul-realization. It is a work in progress rather than some final event. I also look upon the Love Age phases as a journey or destiny without a finish line.

Currently, I see myself primarily experiencing Soul-realization and primarily operating in the co-creating phase while shifting into oneness-creating. These latter phases will be discussed in the next chapter. These are the phases of creating needed for the Love Age to mature.

Figure 11.2

> **SUGGESTED QUESTIONS FOR PERSONAL AND GROUP DISCUSSION**
>
> 1. Have you ever had an experience where the mind had serious limitations in helping you create a spiritual solution?
> 2. Have you recognized most of your ego habits?
> 3. Soul has powers for co-creating (awareness, focusing attention, and distributing love and wisdom). Which one is your best spiritual strength?
> 4. Have you experienced life as being purposeful?
> 5. Have you changed your old life plan and started co-creating a Love Age plan?
> 6. Do you observe your life with objective soul awareness?
> 7. Have you ever had a feeling of emptiness about life that helped push you forward in your spiritual growth?
> 8. How do you use divine love or divine wisdom?
> 9. Have you found that discussion groups help you understand more than you would understand alone?
> 10. Do you recognize the divine self dwelling in you as the "true me?"
> 11. Are you ego-realized?
> 12. Are you soul-realized?

Chapter Twelve

Love Age-creating Phases

My mother told me a joke about an older lady named Rose. Rose attended church faithfully and tried her best to understand Pastor Tim's sermons. One Sunday morning, Pastor Tim spoke about the "hereafter." He encouraged his flock to place their attention on the "hereafter," for this was the realm of spirit and God.

After the service was over, Pastor Tim stood at the front door, greeting his parishioners as they left church. When Rose approached the Pastor, she said, "You know, the older I get, the more I think about the hereafter."

Pastor Tim reached out to shake her hand while saying, "Rose, I'm so thankful to hear you say that."

It was then that Rose put her hand on her chin, as though she was pondering something, and said, "Almost every time I go down to my basement, I'm always asking myself, what am I *here after*?"

***

Most people in their ego consciousness are as confused about where their attention should be focused as Rose was. Their ego eyes focus only on the realities of the physical and mental worlds. Those that are spiritual and use the eyes of Soul know that they must view the reality of both the physical and spiritual worlds. If we are to learn to do LoveAge-creating, the "hereafter" focus is part of life. This is where the spiritual powers of wisdom and love originate.

LoveAge-creating Phases

In the LoveAge-creating phases, attention needs to be refocused from being primarily on the material world or ego consciousness to being on the world of spirit, where Soul and the Divine have the powers to transform life with love. Tapping into the power of Soul is a major transition in which Soul consciously controls the mind, emotions, and imagination and operates in a co-creative partnership or oneness with the Divine to create life.

LoveAge-creating is an *inside/outside process* of creating. In comparison to ego-creating, which relies on trying to change things on the outside, Love Age-creating is primarily done from the inside. You use intentions, thoughts, feelings, and imagination and allow the Divine to create what is good-for-All.

The transition between the material and spirit worlds is subtle, and, at times, it's difficult to know what is going on. It is also more difficult to define clear-cut phases. Ego-creating tends to be more linear, where you progress from me-creating to other-creating. LoveAge-creating, on the other hand, tends to be more of a feedback model or a circular model of progress. Co-creating, oneness-creating, and soul-realization are interdependent. I, therefore, found it more difficult to know where I fit in the phases of LoveAge-creating than I did with ego-creating.

I have found that there is a strong interconnection between being soul-realized and being able to co-create. It seems that they almost progress at the same time and greatly depend on each other for further empowering with love.

Co-creating Phase

You might have heard co-creating mentioned before, since the idea has become more popular recently, but some of its basic concepts have been around for thousands of years. Since there is a new consciousness shift toward partnering with the Divine and away from the father/child relationship and self-empowerment, this phase for creating has become more important for the Love Age.

> *Co-creating Is a Way to Help Create the Love Age*

Instead of having less or no power, as a child would in the father/child relationship of creating, you as a co-creator function as a partner with the freedom and responsibilities to help create the direction your personal life or world will take. Some of you are probably thinking, *Who does Tommy think he is? He's an egomaniac, thinking he's a partner with the Divine and able to help direct the destiny of the world.*

While in the ego consciousness, I wasn't a partner with the Divine. I held the illusion that I was separate form others and from the Divine. I thought I was a victim of their creations or that I was the mighty pompous self-creator using ego tactics to get what I wanted. Mostly, I felt like a helpless, victimized child without much in the way of creative powers.

When I realized that I was Soul or the Divine Self, I knew that I had the divine attributes of freedom of choice and had responsibilities in the co-creative process. If I choose to have freedom of choice, it gave me the opportunity to be a co-creating partner. I had responsibilities for initiating and deciding the direction of the creative process that would help to bring about my personal and collective intentions for the world.

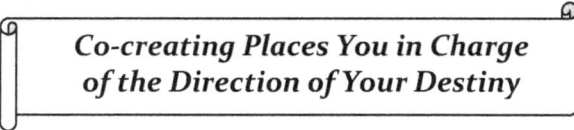

Co-creating Places You in Charge of the Direction of Your Destiny

Co-creators also need to understand that the Divine uses other Souls as partners in order to help materialize intentions. For example, you will most likely have a special co-creative or spiritual partner who is significant for this lifetime and who will help you co-create your destiny. You also have partners helping from inner spiritual worlds.

If you haven't realized who my spiritual partner is by this time, it is my wife, Audrey. I feel certain that we decided before we were born that we would serve as each other's spiritual partners. When I look back over our lives, it is amazing how we arrived together at the point where we are now. She did a lot of pulling and pushing, and I did some too.

See Figure 12.1 for an illustration of the co-creating phase. In comparison to the ego-creating phases, the creative-threes change from the "me" or ego self to the Divine Self. "Others" become communities of love, and "God" is the Loving Source or the Divine. God or the Divine hasn't changed throughout any of the phases, but our perceptions of the Divine change, especially when the LoveAge-creating phases are realized. The arrows pointing in two directions indicate the interdependent relationships of the three basic creative elements, which are in a state of partnership.

The basic motivation is to do what is good-for-All, and the Divine has the responsibility to guide us to do it. The Divine Self is responsible for observing and stopping the ego's reactions, initiating the good-for-All intention, focusing on the intention to

Figure 12.1

CO-CREATING PHASE

LOVING SOURCE

Divine Self   **Communities of Love**

Motivated to create what's Good-for-All. Divine is a partner providing divine love and wisdom while Soul consciously initiates intentions, energizes them, and allows the Divine to co-create what's best for all.

energize it, and allowing the Divine to guide its co-creation. The communities of love or others are responsible for following the guidance of the Divine, so they can help with the creation of your and their intentions too.

Co-creating Intends and Does What's Good-for-All

Since I am going to discuss how to do the co-creative way more extensively in another book, I am not going to go into any details about it now. Co-creation is a process of consciously co-creating with the Divine's guidance and with other spiritual partners, for the good-of-All. It is a shift from having little or no good-for-All creating powers to being a partner with a lot to say about the direction of your own personal destiny as well as that of the world.

By transforming our powers from the ego to Soul by means of co-creating, we will help bring about the Love Age by one Soul at a time changing itself. Co-creating combines the most important power tools of love in order to change your life. Its three basic tools are summarized in this way: Recognize It; Replace It; and Allow It.

This is primarily where I am in my spiritual consciousness. I am now gaining most of my understanding as well as my experiences in the co-creating phase, but intending to be a oneness-creator.

Do you see yourself as a co-creator?

Co-creating is a Step on the Path to Oneness

LoveAge-creating Phases

Ego empowerment has a polarizing effect and creates for the good-of-me or for others. Co-creating, on the other hand, is a more conscious way of directing life with intentions, a way which is better for All and which is more responsible for creating desired circumstances than is ego-creating. It is also in tune with the Divine's purpose of co-creating for the good-of-All. It will most likely be the predominant way of creating the Love Age for some time to come. However, there is a higher form of LoveAge-creating than co-creating. It is oneness-creating.

Oneness-creating Phase

Oneness-creating is a phase of consciousness that I aspire to reach. I mainly have a mental understanding of oneness. I have had a few experiences that were glimpses of what it must be like to have the oneness consciousness. It's at the deepest levels of receiving and giving love, working in harmony with the Divine, receiving the peace that passes all understanding, being joyful, being free, and knowing the wisdom of Divine stillness. Its motivation is oneness-with-All.

A representation of oneness-creating is illustrated on the next page in Figure 12.2. The Loving Source, or the Divine smiley face, encompasses the Divine Self and the communities of love in a blanket of love, peace, joy, unity, and wisdom. Creating arises out of this oneness with All that knows what's good-for-All and creates with the greatest love for All.

The ego-realization and soul-realization phases helped free me from the material, mental, and emotional worlds of the ego. These reside in the mental and emotional subtle energy bodies or in the energy fields that surround the physical body. At the level of oneness-creating, we are free of reincarnation and *karma*, have learned most of our lessons of love, are at home in the physical and spiritual worlds, are masters of using energy from the Divine, are energy healers, and exist in a consciousness of unity with ALL.

Figure 12.2

ONENESS-CREATING PHASE
(*Create with Divine Oneness and Unity*)

LOVING SOURCE

Divine Self   **Communities of Love**

Beginning of Oneness is Shifting Attention to Soul

Oneness-creating is a phase in which one becomes a master of all of the Love Age empowerment tools, mastering thoughts, feelings, and imagination, and uniting with Divine stillness and with the One. In comparison to co-creating, oneness-creating is already immersed in the wisdom of the Divine and does not need to wait for communications about what are good-for-All intentions and actions. It is consequently a faster way of creating.

I have been placing a lot of attention on experiencing the oneness of the Divine through affirmations, through feeling the state of being one, and through hearing the wisdom of Divine Stillness in meditation and in my daily life. If I'm doing meditation or affirmations during the day, I first focus my attention at the top of my head, where the crown *chakra* or Soul resides. I have a useful affirmation, which I repeat slowly, and I feel deeply each of the qualities of oneness within Soul as I focus my attention on each one. It is as follows:

I'm one with Soul. (pause & feel it within)
I feel its love, (pause & feel it within)
Its peace, (pause & feel it within)
Its joy, (pause & feel it within)
Its freedom, (pause & feel it within)
Its wisdom of stillness. (pause & listen to the stillness)

The way to oneness is mainly through being love, since oneness is love. This does not refer to the personalized love of the ego consciousness but to the divine love of Soul. When you intend and do what is good-for-All, it is the love of All where the All is the One. Oneness involves loving more and more and more until you become the One. Love is what the Divine, the One, and Soul are. Most of the time during the day, I just repeat and feel I'm LOVE.

> **Oneness is the State of Being Divine Love**

This union with the Divine or Soul and with all life is the most important aspect of this phase. It helps us realize the heights of what it means to be spiritual and to apply it to everyday life. Oneness-creating arises from the oneness consciousness and is the quickest and highest spiritual form of creating. In this phase, we transform from being a partner (co-creator) to being one with the Divine, with all life, with nature, as well as with the universe. We become a powerhouse of love for All.

At this level, one becomes a master of spirituality and creativity, able to serve the Divine to the fullest, to use oneness-creating, and to help guide others to these heights of spirituality. There are few who have reached this height of LoveAge-creating, but their numbers are growing. Each of you has the power within you to do it, if you have the love and commitment it takes and the patience to wait for the grace of the Divine to gift it to you.

Is it your intention to be a oneness-creator???

You're a LoveAge Creator of One

Earlier, I mentioned the advertisement of an "Army of One." I never quite understood it, since an army's effectiveness rests on large numbers of soldiers obeying orders. An army is based on a top-down structure in which soldiers obey their officers. That ad seemed to be false advertising.

But when it comes to oneness, each of us is truly a Love Age creator of one. No organization or membership in a religion, no amount of good works, no belief or powerful faith, no reading of a sacred book, no spiritual leader, prayers, or anything external to you will give you oneness. It is something you choose, intend, experience, do, be, and live. It ultimately comes down to you and me making and living the spiritual choices of love, which flow

LoveAge-creating Phases

from the inner love and peace arising out of the harmony of oneness. We were given the gift of freedom of choice by the Loving Source to allow us to choose our own spiritual destinies. Ultimately, oneness will be a gift given by the Divine at the appropriate time.

LoveAge-creating uses one's intentions to change oneself and to be an example of love rather than trying to change others. You can serve as an example of love, peace, and joy that others want to live too. Just be a spirituality of one, and by your example, the world will also want to change to be like you. As you progress spiritually, creating stops being an activity outside of you and evolves from within the oneness.

Just because you are a spirituality of one, it doesn't mean you are alone. You have a support group that is beyond your imagination especially the ones on the inner spiritual dimensions. Many people believe that angels or spiritual guides are present at every hour of the day and night to help them. When I'm soul aware, I realize this help and give it my gratitude. The love and wisdom of Soul, Divine Energy, and Divine Source are also there to help.

Even on the outer material world, you have spiritual partners or earth angels who are here to help you realize oneness. Others whom you might think of as your enemies are here also to help give lessons so you will grow spiritually. There are spiritual giants and spiritual leaders from the past as well as some living today who are here to help you on your path of oneness.

All you have to do is to ask for this help, trust it, and allow the Divine and your spiritual partners do their parts. Spirituality of one has the best help service desk available, and it's waiting for your intentions, questions, commitments, as well as doing your part.

In summary, ego-creating is where you are either a disempowered victim (e.g., a victim of luck, of God's wrath, or of circumstances created by others) or a self-empowered creator of doing what is good-for-me or for others. When you shift from ego-creating to LoveAge-creating, your true creative power of love is realized. Co-empowerment and the empowerment of oneness maximize the power of love that often lies dormant within you.

It doesn't matter at what point you find yourself on the creative power journey; just take the next empowerment step. Your intentions to be a creator of love and to turn ego habits into loving actions will make your life much more fulfilling. The most important things you can do to move toward creating more love are as follows: increase your personal energy vibrations of love from within, be more and more in charge of the ego, know that your essence is love, co-create what's good-for-All, be a partner with the Divine, and eventually live in the consciousness of oneness.

The next three chapters will discuss the transition from the Ego Age to the Love Age. Ego-realization, soul-realization, co-creating, and oneness-creating are necessary and important for you and for the transformation of the world.

Figure 12.2

SUGGESTED QUESTIONS FOR PERSONAL AND GROUP DISCUSSION

1. Have you experienced any of the Love Age-creating phases?
2. Have you committed to being a co-creator?
3. Are you a co-creator?
4. Have you ever had an inner experience that gave you guidance about your destiny?
5. Is it your desired destiny to be a oneness-creator?
6. Are you a Love Age creator of one?
7. Do you love more and more and more to be One?
8. Have you ever felt the oneness of love, peace, joy, freedom, and Divine stillness?

SHIFT V

Ego Age to Love Age

How important is it for you to be a LoveAge-creator? Is there a major evolutionary change in consciousness happening now? Some believe that a major shift from the Ego Age to the Love Age has begun and will continue to grow, depending on yours and on others' commitment to it. Others have decided that the end of time is at hand and believe it will happen in 2012. What do you think is happening?

Chapter Thirteen

Is the World Ending or Shifting?

Mary had just gotten off the school bus after a half day attending her kindergarten class. Her mother saw tears in her eyes as she stepped off the bus. "Mary, what's wrong? Why are you crying?"

"Johnny told me his father said the end of time is coming and there will be a lot of deaths. If there is no time, I'll not know when to wake up, eat, or go to the school bus. What will happen to my Cinderella watch? He also said the world will be destroyed and I'm afraid to die."

Mary's mother wiped the tears from her eyes as they walked home. "Mary, you don't have to worry about time going away or the world being destroyed. There are some people that believe that, but your dad and I don't. In fact, if people like you and I choose it, the world will be a much happier, loving, and peaceful place to live. Wouldn't that be nice?"

"Oh yes. Does that mean I can keep my Cinderella watch?"

***

Many see no hope for the ego world, other than its destruction. Some have been fearing and predicting its ending for thousands of years. Others, on the other hand, are more positive and believe things are and will improve.

What do you believe about the possible outcome of today's world?

Throughout this book, I have concluded that the ego consciousness with its focus on conflict, polarization, fear, warring technology, greed, intolerance, and other destructive reactions may lead to the world's destruction. It is one of the options facing humankind today. In addition, religions and others have been predicting the end of time, and it has become an intensely discussed topic in 2012 because of the Mayan calendar ending during that year.

If you are reading this book in 2013, you'll know for sure that 2012 was not the time for the ending of the world. But I'll assure you that there will be groups of people who will continue to believe it will happen at another date sometime in the future. They have been doing this for centuries and will most likely continue making these predictions.

No one knows what is going to happen in the future since humans have the freedom to choose their destiny. Ending the world is an option, but so is making the world a better place to live with a consciousness based on love. We are the ones who will make that choice.

Throughout my life, I changed beliefs about whether the world was ending or shifting, which I will address in this chapter. I will also discuss why the end of time has become a topic of keen interest and what will most likely happen according to my observations, beliefs, and desires. The focus of this chapter and book is not limited to just what will happen in 2012, but it has a far more broader interest in what will happen during the Twenty-first Century.

This book is based on a more optimistic view about what has been, is currently, and will be happening in the world. Therefore, 2012 is considered an important year for a shift in consciousness with many more years for us to learn and to create with love.

End of Time Beliefs

Since movies, TV, and other media have predicted the destruction or the end of the world in 2012, many have wondered if this will actually happen. My daughter, BJ, who manages medical clinics, told me that one of the doctors working in one of her clinics asked what she thought about 2012. I also heard about a high school teacher who was asked by students about 2012. People of all ages are growing anxious about whether the world will end in 2012.

This issue of the world ending has been around for centuries. Since the first century AD, some Christians have been hoping for the end of time when evil will finally be defeated. In April of 2011, I saw a prediction of the second coming of Christ on a billboard in Sacramento. It read, "The Lord Is Coming—May 11, 2011." I wondered what that was all about, and I discovered later after searching the Internet that Harold Camping, a Christian preacher, claimed that the "Rapture" or the end of time would happen on May 21, 2011. He and others have been setting dates for the end of time since Jesus's crucifixion, but the dates come and go without anything happening as Camping's did. Regardless of Camping's unsuccessful predictions, I've heard he has been dancing and singing on his way to the bank with millions in his pockets.

The word "rapture" does not appear anywhere in the Bible. The idea was instead a religious dogma started during the seventeenth century, when many believed that true believing Christians would be saved and taken in bodily form directly to heaven (i.e., rapture). Nonbelievers at the end would be left behind to fight evil in the battle of Armageddon. If this isn't a good-for-me Christian belief, I don't know what is.

When I was a teenage member of the Methodist Church, they didn't discuss much about the end of time or about Armageddon. I knew about it, but I thought it was thousands of years in the future. It wasn't until I read Edgar Cayce's predictions about the ocean engulfing the western coast that I became concerned about large-scale destruction in America.

Feared Large-scale Destruction in America

Cayce predicted that large-scale destruction would happen in 1958 and beyond because of our consciousness affecting earth's natural systems, but it did not happen. I wrote off the failed prediction as another instance of psychics having difficulty predicting specific dates since they worked on the spiritual dimensions where past and future time doesn't exist. In addition, humans have the freedom of choice, and their choices affect what happens in the future, which creates a great deal of uncertainty for those predicting future events. Who can predict what humans will choose now or at some time in the future?

The future is highly unpredictable; even the Divine does not know what choices we humans will make since we have freedom of choice. The Divine also does not intervene, so we must accept the consequences of our choices. Our cumulative choices are what determine the future, and that fact creates a great deal of uncertainty for those who want to predict it. In addition to reading about Cayce's predictions, I also had my own personal experience about the possibility of devastating destruction, and this poured more energy into my fears.

***

Sometime around 1993 or 1994, I watched a TV program about the time track. The guest led the audience in a time travel exercise, and I followed along. I closed my eyes, and she told us to select a year in the future, to view what we wanted to see. I decided to see the United States in 2025. I believed in the time track, but I didn't think I would ever have an experience seeing a potential future.

Almost instantly, I saw myself high above the United States somewhere over Missouri or Arkansas and looking north. I looked to the east coast, and everything seemed about the same as it is now. When I looked to the west, I saw the ocean covering the states from California to Washington and on into Colorado or Kansas. I couldn't see exact state boundaries, but the ocean covered most of western America, and it looked like a giant U-shaped indentation. I also saw three or four volcanoes with red-hot lava spewing from them on the northern rim that were probably situated somewhere near Wyoming or Montana. This destruction appeared to have happened sometime before 2025, since Americans had already returned to what seemed to be normal living.

I then zoomed in closely to a city somewhere in the Midwest that might have been Chicago. There were tall silver skyscrapers towering into the sky that looked something like the Transamerica Building in San Francisco. The people were wearing silver metallic suits that made them look like they might have been from outer space. But they looked like us, and they didn't have to wear breathing apparatus over their heads to live in our atmosphere.

When I returned to consciousness, I thought that the experience was just something my imagination conjured up. But sometime around 1994 or 1995, my wife was working as a cardiac rehabilitation nurse, and a patient told her about Gordon Michael Scallion's predictions of earth changes. During a later appointment, he gave her a map that showed the extent of Scallion's predictions. When she showed it to me, my mouth dropped about a mile. The western states were submerged under the ocean just as I had seen them in my time track experience.

Gordon Michael Scallion's predictions added additional fuel to my fears of devastating earth changes. He predicted that the changes would happen in stages, but his first prediction for 1997 didn't happen. I rationalized that it was another psychic having trouble with predicting dates because of the difference of time on the inner and the changing consciousness of humans.

My experiences suggested that there would be widespread destruction, but not the end of humans as a species. It made me wonder. Where was the safest place to live in the United States?

***

Many fundamentalist Christian religions believe in the Armageddon prophecies, which add to this hysteria of destruction. The potential of nations or terrorists using nuclear weapons adds additional fuel to the fear of mass destruction. The more violent climate and earth changes are also adding to this hysteria.

The History Channel TV programs, too, add fuel to the end of the world hysteria. These trumped-up fears are probably good for the network's ratings but are not good for the positive consciousness needed to bring about the age of love. On February 15, 2010, I watched a program on the History Channel about the seven potential threats to humans' survival, listed in order from the most likely to the least likely potential source of destruction. The documentary makers suggested that the worst threat was climate change, followed by a pandemic or biological warfare, nuclear war, asteroids hitting Earth, a super volcano exploding, a black hole engulfing us, and killer gamma rays from a sunburst. Did you notice that the top three threats were those that humans created or helped create, which stems from ego choices? It seems we have become our own worst enemies according to the History Channel.

> *The Ego in Control of Technology*
> *Has Become Our Own Worst Enemy*

There is one thing that is a certainty about the end of the world, as Charles Schulz, the cartoonist of Peanuts, pointed out. Fearing that the world will end today is useless, since Australia will have already experienced tomorrow.

Is the World Ending or Shifting?

What Is the Importance of 2012?

The Mayan calendar will end on December 21, 2012, which marks the end of the Mayan Great Cycle and the start of another one. On that day, the winter solstice will occur, but it will be a rare one since it has been 26,000 years since the solar system, sun, and our planet were aligned exactly as they will be with the center of our Milky Way galaxy.

John Major Jenkins, one of the most well-known independent researchers of the Mayan culture, disagrees with those who say that the calendar's ending date is a prediction of the end of the world. The anthology, *The Mystery of 2012*, edited by Tami Simon, contains Jenkins's article, "The Origins of the 2012 Revelation." In the article, he says the Mayans saw "the galactic alignment of era—2012 as a great opportunity for spiritual seekers to reconnect with the source of perennial wisdom. We shouldn't wait until 2012, for we are in alignment zone now (1980–2016). The time, as always, is now." His understanding of the Mayan prediction of a new age is what I have been referring to as the Love Age.

> *Mayans Used 2012 as a Beginning of a New Age of Spirituality*

Scientists have observed that along with this rare alignment will come some other potential physical earth changes. Researchers have found that the magnetic poles are changing and that the weakening of strength of the earth's magnetic pull affects consciousness since both consist of electrical and magnetic energy. According to the *Kryon* books, this alignment of the magnetic grid is happening to allow for the increase in consciousness needed for the new age of love.

It has been theorized that the weaker the magnetic pull, the more consciousness can be open to change. Since the west coast of America is one of the weakest magnetic areas, it may be a potential hotbed for change. This could help bring about faster changes in the world's consciousness and could help launch the Love Age into a higher gear.

What is the Significance of December 21, 2012?

The Mayans established that the date for the ending of the 26,000-year cycle is December 21, 2012. The 2012 date is a Mayan calculation using ancient means to establish when the earth will align with the galaxy and when the old age ends and another begins. I agree with the Mayans that a new age is in the process of coming, since I have observed changes in my own and in others' spiritual consciousness since the 1960s and especially since 1998, but I doubt that the December date of 2012 is the exact date of a new age.

Modern scientific measurements have established that the galactic alignment has already occurred in 1998, which means the alignment has been going on for some time. The Mayans missing it by 14 years out of a 26,000-year cycle without modern instrumentation doesn't seem to be a big deal. Pinpointing an exact date within a 26,000-year cycle really isn't all that important. According to *Kryon*, trying to do so is to get caught up in the problem of earth's linear time structure, when in actuality there is only the eternal now. Since we are on clock time here on earth, deciding on December 21, 2012 as the beginning of the new age can be acceptable for helping humans with their need to have beginnings and endings for things.

The year 2012 can become a significant beginning for a shift to a greater spirituality rather than an ending date for our destruction. Hopefully, we continue to improve up to December 2012 and beyond. John Major Jenkins believed 2012 was the midpoint of a spiritual change in consciousness that would last for a century between 1962 and 2062. This may be a more accurate assessment since the 1960s did start a significant change in consciousness. Unfortunately, the baby boomer generation's desire for a love-based society reversed its priorities and the lifestyles of these people became major contributors to the ego consciousness of today's world along with its economic problems, conflicts, drug usage, polarizations, and unhappiness. The boomers and the rest of us took a step forward and I'm not sure how many steps back.

Should the beginning of the Love Age be set at 1962, 1998, 2012, or at some other date? I would prefer to think it started in the 1960s when there were changes in racial and gender equality, when people taught "love, not war" and nonviolence, and when other love-oriented states of consciousness occurred that changed people as well as ego institutions. This was the time I personally moved my own consciousness into nonviolence and good-for-other love. This period also initiated a broader search for spirituality that started the merger of Western and Eastern religions. Today, this merger is producing fruit for the consciousness of spirituality. I saw on an outdoor church sign, "God's not looking for spiritual nuts, but for spiritual fruit." I believe this is happening now, and at a faster pace.

Since there has been a great deal of collective consciousness focused on 2012 as a transition date, it would be wise to let it serve as a midpoint for the Love Age, which marks a significant moment when the world's spiritual consciousness reaches a higher point. The number of people starting to be more loving will most likely significantly increase up to this point and especially beyond. The period between 2012 and 2016 will most likely experience a significant increase in the power of love.

In 2012, there will possibly be no noticeable significant event to mark a changed spiritual consciousness since this sort of change cannot be seen by the physical eyes except for the behavioral changes it might produce. Sensitive spiritual people may feel the heightened vibrations, but most will see nothing, nor will they feel any changes taking place. This is why a collective celebration of your personal commitment and changes would be useful for focusing attention on love and peace at that time.

Your Creative Power of Love

It is easy to see today's escalation of ego conflicts, but many do not realize that this escalation is an ego reaction to the changes that are occurring. The daily news broadcasts are almost exclusively negative, which keeps attention on the ego consciousness, while the positive is hardly noticed. Humanity has to start recognizing the changes in love, freedom, and peace that are going on in the world and to become part of that consciousness. The desires for freedom and peace in Africa and the Middle East have been examples of the increase in conflict arising from a desire for freedom, equality, and a changed consciousness. The protests in America are also indications of this changing consciousness.

The reality of the Love Age can only be in your thoughts, feelings, heart, and imagination, and that's how social reality is created. If this is your reality for 2012 and beyond, it will then be the reality for the Love Age as well. You have the power to determine the meaning of 2012 and the years that follow by your choices of being more loving and committing to be a co-creator of love while joining with others in this commitment.

Since the beginning of the Love Age is a relative date, you could also view it from a personal perspective rather than from a collective one. The beginning of the age of love could be when you decide to be a more loving being and to make a commitment to co-create love or oneness. For me, my change in consciousness started in the early 1960s.

What date would you set as the beginning of your commitment to being a loving being?

I experienced 1998 as a time when a significant movement in my spiritual consciousness happened. In 1998, I started writing this book and made more spiritual progress after that date than I had made during the first 60 years of my life. The galactic alignment most likely helped increase the higher vibrations of spiritual energy that I needed for unfoldment. I believe the effects of the alignment and the increase in energy that significantly increased in 1998 will continue to create more significant increases up to 2016 and beyond. This will make it easier for me and for you to become more enlightened beings of love.

Have you experienced a change in your consciousness of love since 1998?

Experiencing Higher Energy Vibrations

On the path of tuning into divine presence, oneness, soul awareness, and Divine Stillness, I have periods of strong and weak connections. My spiritual partnership between my wife, myself, and the Divine in the latter months of 2009 and early 2010 went through a rough period.

My wife had taken two classes in *Reiki* healing at the University of California, Davis Medical Center and she was enthusiastic about the new direction in her life. I had always had an intuitive feeling that she was a healer beyond what she did as a nurse.

In the summer of 2009, she had a past life regression. In her first experience, she was an American Indian boy, and she felt free and happy in that lifetime. In the next life experience, it began with an agonizing experience of her feet and legs on fire, and it became so painful that she had to be quickly brought out of the past life regression. She felt she had gone back to a past life experience of being burnt at the stake for her healing practices. It put a strong fear in her that the same thing might happen again if she became a healer.

I suspected that this experience changed her enthusiasm about becoming a healer, during the fall and winter months of 2009. She didn't do much healing for the family, and she stopped reading books about it. At times, her ego reactions flared up, which tended to drown out her compassionate ways. During these times, it became more difficult to live with her. I had a feeling that her Soul had become restless and discontent with the direction her life wasn't taking. She tried to escape by watching TV or by being an Internet grandma, but these things did nothing for her soul's inner restlessness.

In February of 2010, she started reading some of her *Reiki* books and other spiritual books again. She even decided to attend the Sacramento book discussion group with me. Things were beginning to improve on the home front too. She was getting back to her old compassionate ways.

In March, she decided to take the third level *Reiki* class. I drove Audrey to the *Reiki* master's house where she talked to her about the class. While I was waiting for her to finish, I began to have a high volume of spiritual energy flowing through me. After the meeting, it increased when we went to a store that sold crystals. Crystals were one of Audrey's new interests, since she had had a healing of a blockage in her trachea by a healer using crystals. While Audrey was in the store, she said she felt that the energy there made her feel like she was floating on her feet. She bought some crystals, and on our way home, the energy continued to flow through both of us.

I told her that our spiritual partnership was transforming into a higher spiritual level, and she agreed. Later that night, the energy was still flowing, and I couldn't fall asleep. My wife had the same problem. This will often happen when you become a more open channel for Divine Energy until you learn to balance the increased flow of vibrating energy into your body and life.

This increased flow of spirit reminded me of the time when lightning hit a tree in my yard. It knocked out the TV and the phones. This increased electrical surge put our communications out of balance, and they didn't work anymore. A lightning strike is sort of like what an increase in spiritual vibrations will do to your body; it will put you out of balance. This is the reason that small spiritual steps are usually easier to handle than large spiritual jolts of energy vibrations. But I'll take it any way I can get it.

Let us now return to the rest of the story about the increase in spiritual energy. My wife has a clock that projects the digital time on the ceiling of the bedroom, and the last time I remember seeing it was at 4:30 a.m. The next morning, we were to

Is the World Ending or Shifting?

attend the Sacramento discussion group and discuss *The Power of Now* by Eckhart Tolle at 9:30 a.m. When it was time to awaken, both of us decided not to attend the meeting. We were too tired. I rolled over and went back to sleep. When I finally awoke that morning, I looked up at the ceiling and saw that the time was 11:11 a.m. My jaws dropped, and I couldn't wait to get up to tell my wife about this seeing-sign.

About four months earlier, I had read the book, *The Great Shift*, in which Lee Carroll had channeled some messages of *Kryon*. My wife had ordered some more of the *Kryon* books just before she had gone to the *Reiki* teacher, and I was reading *Kryon Book Eleven, Lifting the Veil*. I remembered reading about the significance of seeing the 11:11 time as a sign, but I didn't remember exactly what it meant.

The first thing I did was to turn to the book's index and read the various sections referring to 11:11. The number one represented new beginnings, and the number combination, 11:11, represented the *new higher energy* that was helping my wife and me to unfold and to bring about a new age of love and peace. The numbers also represented *illumination*. This all related to our current experiences with increased spiritual vibrations. I also realized that this was the number symbol that referred to the Love Age, which I had been writing about.

The 11:11 was a seeing-sign to let me know that the increased energy my wife and I were feeling was connected to the spiritual energy of the new age. Sometimes I had wondered if anything was really happening spiritually, and this seeing-sign came along to give me additional verification that, yes, something indeed was happening.

There was another insight to learn from the 11:11 seeing-sign. In the *Kryon* book, I also read, "It is not a repeated coincidence when you see the 11:11 on your clocks. It is a 'wink' from Spirit to remind you why you are here."

I began to regret my decision about not attending the discussion group that morning. It was my responsibility to be there and to serve as a co-student for sharing spirit's wisdom. The Love Age is not something that will come lightly or without effort. The *Kryon* books mention that we may sometimes go to bed tired and awaken tired, but it is still our responsibility to help give birth to the new love energy.

This seeing-sign was also a confirmation that I was getting help on the inner. The *Kryon* books keep mentioning that in the spiritual worlds, we have an inner family of entities that some call angels, inner guides, or spiritual guides, and that they are always with us and helping us. Much of what they do I have no awareness of. But it is comforting to know that I am not alone in becoming spiritual or in helping to try to bring about the Love Age. Our guides and the Divine work 24/7 to help us do it.

A Higher Consciousness Is Evolving

World leaders increasingly desire to negotiate conflicts and differences rather than to fight. People are protesting in the streets for their freedoms and for economic security, and there is a concern among world leaders that ruthless authoritarian leaders should be held accountable for their violent actions. People are choosing to leave old religions and to be more spiritual, to live in tune with the principles of love, and to live in more harmony with others and the environment. These changes are raising the consciousness level here on Earth.

I do not fear being burnt at the stake for my spiritual beliefs. The world has become more tolerant toward other races, to women, religions, gays, the aged, and ethnic minorities. World circumstances are forcing us to cooperate more on a global level. The world is heading in the right direction through gradual steps, but there are still a lot more steps to take. It is also likely that we will often take three steps forward and one back.

***

During recent massive natural disasters, the compassion of people flowed much stronger. A day or so after a tornado occurred in Joplin, Missouri, I eventually managed to talk to Bill, a nephew of mine, whose house had been torn to shreds. I thought he would feel devastated, but instead he told me how amazed he was that people he didn't even know were doing or offering to do things to help him. He was touched by the love and compassion they were showing. He also told me that right after the tornado, he went over to an elderly woman's house next door and to other homes, to lend a helping hand. Many of the neighbors and strangers were helping in whatever way they could. It was interesting that even in times of devastation; the lessons of love are being learned and practiced.

***

It seems odd, but love is growing because of these mass destructions. This is sometimes how love is learned. Most of the good in these times of mass destruction we do not see, especially since the media loves to find what's negative or destructive to air or show on their programs.

If this trend of compassion continues, the 2012 fears of total destruction of the human species, and other similar fears, will have a slim to no chance of materializing. A more positive consciousness has already started to change the ego's tendencies for destruction. The bottom line is that humans must continue to use their conscious intentions to be more loving, in order to prevent the ego consciousness from destroying the world. Since most of the world's problems are self-imposed and are consequences of the ego consciousness, I believe the hearts and spirits of humans will co-create a state of harmony with the environment, with others, and with the Divine.

In *Kryon Book 11*, Lee Carroll wrote that in 1987 Souls in the spiritual dimensions decided that a new energy of peace would prevail. The Armageddon prophesies of the end of the world were therefore not on track to happen anymore, depending on our continual choices of being more loving or spiritual. The world was actually on track to end at a point in time around the turn of the century, but these old prophecies did not materialize, since the consciousness of humans has been improving. The question is whether it will continue to improve.

Learning this, released tons of fears for me about major destruction happening in the world. If I continued to work in a partnership or oneness with the Divine to help increase the spiritual energy vibrations here on earth, I would not have to fear this destruction. The choice is yours and mine. If we continue to raise our own personal consciousness, the transition from the ego to spiritual consciousness will most likely happen.

While writing my book and reading others' books about the possibility of a new age of love, I gradually realized that by changing my own consciousness, I would help change the world's consciousness. The *Kryon* books and Eckhart Tolle's book, *A New Earth,* were especially helpful in changing my fears about monumental destruction. They also helped me realize the importance of changing myself to add another changed consciousness for world peace.

You're probably thinking, "Hold on, Tommy, just look at all the conflict and violence that is going on in today's world," and you would be right. We are in a crucial period of transition between the Ego Era and the Spiritual Era of evolution. I will discuss in the next chapter the way in which we are in a jump-state period of evolution between these two eras. In this transition phase, it is true that conflicts, protests, and polarizations are increasing, which is easy to see and hear since these events are in our nation's media on a daily basis. What we do not see is that, at the same time, people and the world are cooperating and becoming more loving. It is, therefore, the worst of times and the best of times.

Since there are those who are trapped in the ego consciousness and who do not want changes, conflicts and polarizations have increased. There will most likely continue to be human conflict, climate changes, volcanoes erupting, and earthquakes like we are experiencing now, but they will be far

Is the World Ending or Shifting?

less destructive than what we would have experienced if the consciousness had not improved.

I began to realize that we have the power, as co-creators, to transform the world into a new age of love. My fear of devastating destruction turned into a passion to help transform my ego consciousness to help bring about the Love Age. I found my purpose for being here on Earth.

Have you found your purpose for being here???

If you allow your consciousness to choose to fear the world's ending in 2012 or at any other time, the energy law of matching, where the universe matches the state of your consciousness, will help draw those circumstances to you and the world. Please, place your attention on a world where all of us are co-creators of love and are living in a world of peace, joy, and freedom.

> *The Love Age Is Co-created by One Changed Consciousness at a Time*

Will the world be destroyed in 2012 or beyond? It's not likely, but it is still a possibility if enough people do not continue to choose to change their consciousness to be more spiritual and loving.

In this chapter, I have discussed the question of when the Love Age will happen. I have indicated that this age has a higher probability of becoming a reality than does the destruction of the world in 2012 or beyond. As far as I'm concerned, the Love Age has already started sometime around the early 1960s, and that 2012 will stand as a midpoint for a potential significant increase in the shift of this consciousness. As the consciousness has changed to this point, there has been an increase in conflict and polarization, which means that we are experiencing a time of conflict as well as a time of increased love.

What happens in 2012 and beyond will be determined by how many of you commit to being loving beings. The future is not set in stone, but it will be determined by each one of your decisions to be more loving. If you are reading this book after 2012, you'll know that there is a stronger probability we are on our way to the Love Age.

The next chapter will focus on placing the Love Age in a broader evolutionary time frame in order to provide further information about the significance of the time in history that we are now experiencing.

Is the World Ending or Shifting?

Figure 13.1

> **SUGGESTED QUESTIONS FOR PERSONAL AND GROUP DISCUSSION**
>
> 1. Do you believe we are in a transition from an Ego Age to a Love Age?
> 2. Do you believe the world will be destroyed in 2012 or will 2012 be a transition toward the Love Age?
> 3. Do you believe we have raised our spiritual awareness high enough so we do not have to go through Armageddon?
> 4. What small thing have you done today to help humanity transition into the Age of Love?
> 5. What do you believe is the significance of 2012?
> 6. Do you believe anything significant will happen on December 21, 2012?
> 7. Have you experienced a change in your spiritual growth since 1998?
> 8. Have you ever experienced the 11:11 seeing-sign?
> 9. Have you decided to be a co-creator of love to help give birth to the Love Age?

☺ *Smile* ☺
Since a new age of love seems more likely,
We will be around for a long time if you choose it.

Chapter Fourteen

Evolution of Awareness

Humans are now in the period of a potential major evolutionary jump of awareness into a higher level of love. If enough people change their consciousness to be more loving now, there will be an increased likelihood of this evolutionary jump into the Love Age. Again, this depends on your making a personal decision to be a spiritual being of love and then living it in your everyday life.

This is not a Pollyanna hope, but it has a strong probability of happening if you and others choose it. You are living in a time of great significance that greatly depends on your conscious participation in helping to shift awareness from the Ego Era to a Spiritual Era.

Are you being more loving to increase the likelihood of shifting to a Spiritual Era of love?

Evolution of Awareness

In this book, the words "awareness" and "consciousness" are used interchangeably. When I read in the past about awareness or consciousness, I was confused about the meaning of the terms. I always thought they related to the state of being conscious or unconscious and being able or unable to observe what was going on in life's circumstances or in my external surroundings.

When I was introduced to the concept of a Divine Self, I began to realize that it was not only the physical environment I could be aware of, but that I could also have awareness of inner feelings, ego reactions, and thoughts as well as the wisdom, peace, and love of the spiritual dimensions. I used to think that thoughts were what constituted awareness, but it is instead the consciousness of Soul that causes us to be aware and to have thoughts of awareness or self-awareness. I eventually referred to this as having soul awareness.

In *Stillness Speaks,* by Eckhart Tolle, he referred to consciousness as being various levels of forms. He compared consciousness to the forms that water can manifest, such as gas, liquid, or ice. When I read this, I thought to myself that consciousness was the same as Divine Source, Divine Energy, Divine Self, and all the other subtle body and physical energy material forms. Consciousness was the unmanifested energy flowing out of the Divine Source and manifesting into different forms. Its vibration rates decreased and eventually became the things we can feel and use here on Earth. Consciousness was not only a state, but it was also what gave life its forms.

In Table 14.1, I expand on Tolle's use of water forms, and I compare them to broad categories of consciousness forms, starting with unmanifested energy and moving through those forms to physical level manifestations. Remember, this is only a comparison to help with the understanding of how awareness manifests in different forms. The comparison is not meant to represent an absolute reality, but it can serve as an illustration of how consciousness appears in different forms.

Table 14.1

COMPARISON OF WATER FORMS WITH CONSCIOUSNESS FORMS

FORMS OF WATER	FORMS OF CONSCIOUSNESS
Gas	Pure consciousness (Divine Source & Energy)
Steam	Soul's golden energy field
Snow	Feelings and imagination
Liquid	Mind and thoughts
Ice	Physical matter (body)

[Source: Eckhart Tolle, *Stillness Speaks*, 2003]

In essence, you and I as Soul are pure consciousness or awareness. Consciousness existed before birth; it exists during your lifetime, and it continues to exist after you die. It is who you are as Soul, and it is eternal. Consciousness is pure energy that never ceases to exist, but only changes its forms. It is a divine gift that allows us to co-create the world of materiality.

For a long while, I had no idea that there was an evolution of awareness that was similar to the way the species evolved biologically. It wasn't until I read *The Biology of Belief,* by Bruce H. Lipton, *Spontaneous Evolution,* by Lipton and Steve Bhaerman, and *Earth Dance,* by Elisabet Sahtouris, that this realization unfolded. These writers discussed the evolution of consciousness mainly from the biological and social perspectives.

Eckhart Tolle's books, *Stillness Speaks, The Power of Now,* and *A New Earth,* added deeper insights into the spiritual level of awareness. Finally, in early 2010 I discovered Lee Carroll's books on *Kryon,* which provided additional insights into what was happening with awareness in today's world. I am deeply indebted to these authors for stimulating my thoughts about the evolution of awareness. I added some of my own experiences and observations to theirs in order to provide an overview of what has happened and what might happen with the evolution of awareness.

Figure 14.1, entitled "Evolution of Awareness," depicts the evolutionary eras of the biological and social/technological eras as well as a potential spiritual awareness era. The first two eras evolved over four billion years on the planet. I prefer to think of them as times where physical biological changes primarily affected life's ability to increase awareness.

Now, the social/technological era primary influences humans, which is controlled by the ego consciousness. The spiritual era, which humanity may choose as its next evolution of awareness, is indicated with dashed lines. The move toward this era has at least started to happen, but making it a reality depends on people's conscious choices and actions.

The horizontal axis is the timeline for changes in the awareness that existed for some four billion years. The break in the timeline indicates how the new changes in awareness are happening at a much faster pace in today's world.

The shift from *single cells to community of cells and on to the species* eras were the periods when most biological improvements took place over billions of years. By contrast, the *social/technological era* has been around for only about 100 to 200 thousand years.

Scientists now know that biological evolution did not happen by small gradual biological changes. Species had long periods of stability interspersed with shorter periods of increased conflicts when adjustments to a changing environment were needed. These adjustments happened during relatively short periods of time, followed again by a longer period of stability. These shorter periods of transitions were called jump-start periods. The evolution of awareness had a similar kind of evolutionary pattern.

Evolution of Awareness

We are now in one of those jump-start periods of transitioning between the ego's Social/technological Era and the Spiritual Era.

Figure 14.1

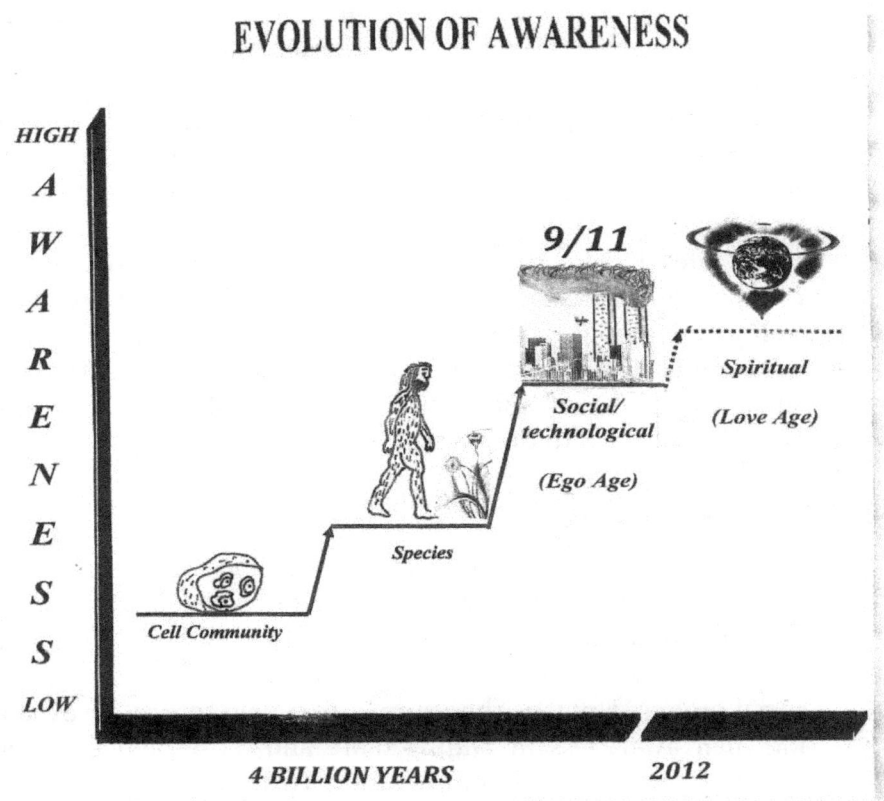

[Sources: Bruce H. Lipton and Steve Bhaerman, *Spontaneous Evolution;* Eckhart Tolle, *A New Earth;* and Lee Carroll's books on *Kryon*]

The left-hand or vertical axis of the chart represents the levels or forms of awareness, with the lowest level being awareness of the physical world of senses and the highest level being awareness of "pure divine consciousness." These levels of awareness were explained in Table 14.1 as it showed some of the possible forms of consciousness or awareness.

Evolutionary Strategies for Increasing Awareness

During the evolution of life forms, they developed strategies to help them be more aware of changing environments in order to adapt to preserve life. There were three basic strategies. One strategy was to make biological changes to *expand the capability of receiving and sharing information*. A second strategy was to *increase the specialization* of bodily functions, knowledge, or social roles. Finally, the strategy of broadening the scope of one's *community* increased the number contributing to awareness as well as increasing the ability to pass on this awareness to other generations. I will not explain the biological awareness strategies, since the focus of this book is on the shift from the social/technological to the spiritual era.

Social/technological Era of Awareness

The Social/technological Era happened when the frontal lobe of the brain of the human species increased its power of the mind to allow its members to use tools or technology, language, and other ways of sharing information between individuals in social groups. Humans then turned to a new source for expanding their awareness by adding more and more people to their groups to expand their communities. This adaptation gave birth to the strategy of the social era where *the size of social communities* such as families, clans, tribes, towns, cities, states, nations, and now global systems increased. Species could now pass knowledge from one generation to another by means of language and by a society's social institutions. This was a strategy for *sharing awareness and teaching it to the next generation or to other groups or nations*. For example, the technology of the Internet increased the speed and amount of information the worldwide community can share.

The expansion of the frontal lobe of the brain also gave humans the capability of self-awareness where they could view themselves as separate egos from others. For the ego to protect itself and increase what it received from the environment, it unfortunately used the *strategy of conflict* to get what's good-for-me. This gave rise to the ego consciousness, which also used the strategy of the *specialization of social roles* such as male/female, father/mother, teacher/student, CEO/secretary, and other relationships to increase specialized awareness or knowledge. This in turn created separateness, intolerance, and conflicts.

The ego relied on dogmatic thoughts and passed its beliefs and values on to members of its society by means of its "institutional me" (i.e., religious, political, economic, family, and educational institutions). The conflicting nature of the ego was embedded in society's institutions, which made them difficult to change.

The Social/technological Era of the ego is highly affected by conflicts rather than by cooperative love, by separation rather than by unity, by war technology rather than by being peaceful, by greedy abundance for the few, and by limited rational and faith-based knowing rather than by all-encompassing divine wisdom. Since the ego has become so dysfunctional and its technology may annihilate humans and other life, it is now at an evolutionary end-point.

Scientists have estimated that of all of the species that have existed since the beginning of life, 99.9 percent of them are extinct today. Extinction is the rule and not the exception. If a species doesn't have the awareness that allows it to adapt and to cooperate at higher levels of wisdom, it most likely becomes a member of the extinct club. Technology has given us the power to control and destroy the world, and the human species overindulges in conflict. This should be a wake-up call since we will not be exempt from a potential extinction. That sure sounds like a harsh reality, and it is a condemnation of the ego consciousness as a potential option for our future.

Within nature and the human body, science has found that the awareness of cooperation is used much more than conflict. Unfortunately, humans have reversed the trend, with conflict being more dominant. This is the nature of the mental ego. Since we are currently in a jump-start period between the Social/technological Era and the Spiritual Era, I hope we learn to do the needed jumping to allow our consciousness to transition into the next era. It's like we are casually trying to walk through the red hot coals of the ego consciousness while we should be leaping out of them and into the Love Age consciousness.

Spiritual Era of Awareness

A strategy based on spiritual awareness is our new hope for resolving the problems that the ego's social/technological era has created and is creating. Fortunately, a higher spiritual consciousness is possible now and is gaining momentum. The important question is, Will you and others continue to choose and use co-creating or oneness-creating to expand LoveAge-creating powers? The *strategy of expanding awareness and receiving guidance from the higher spiritual communities allows us to live with love for the good-of-All and in a true cooperative spirit of oneness.* This will transform the Ego Era into the Spiritual Era where the age of love blossoms.

If this happens, humanity will co-create the Love Age where peace, joy, freedom, and harmony with others and with the environment abound. This outcome requires your conscious choices and actions as a co-creator to help establish this reality.

In the book *Kryon, A New Dispensation, Book 10*, Lee Carroll channeled a message about the urgency of creating peace on earth. Peace is "not only possible, it's probable...to exist is to have peace." In another place, he states that "peace is no longer an option, it is a necessity."

Bruce H. Lipton and Steve Bhaerman believe that the cooperative model of communities of cells in our bodies should serve as a model for a new age. There are approximately 10 trillion cells in your body, which are specialized into organs and a host of 100 trillion microorganisms that help us function. They operate with a high degree of communication, cooperation, unity, and harmony with each other, without your conscious thoughts being involved. They facilitate the means by which the body lives in a healthy and vibrant state of balance. Lipton and Bhaerman, along with other biologists such as Elisabet Sahtouris, agree that the cooperative and harmonious nature of the body is an excellent model of how we should live in the harmony of love with our social and natural environments.

During this jump-start period, the old ego consciousness of individuals, families, education, religion, economy, and government will be fighting a battle and reacting to any changes that threaten the consciousness of what is good-for-me. Consequently, conflicts will continue to exist until we transition out of the jump-start period. Most likely, ego conflicts will gradually subside, but the pace depends on how many live with love for the good-of-All.

> *Pull Out Your Ego Weeds and*
> *Harvest the Fruits of LoveAge-creating*

Some of the changes or shifts in consciousness that you will need to make in order to help bring about the Love Age are described in Table 14.2. Review them; find out how many shifts you have already made and discover the ones you still need to make.

When I talk to others about the coming of the Love Age, they immediately complain about the conflicts existing in today's world, such as the greed of dictators, the rich, and of corporations, the use of war to settle disputes, entrenched beliefs in ego's social institutions, political polarization, and the youth who are on drugs and people who don't want to work. People ask, How can the world be changed when all of this exists?

My answer is that what happens in the world doesn't ultimately depend on anyone except me and you. You are responsible for yourself, and I'm responsible for me. All you need to do is to commit to being the best person of love you can be in order to change your own life and circumstances and to serve as an example for others to change. Just take 30 seconds a day, and ask divine wisdom, *What small thing can I do today to be more loving?*

Are you taking responsibility for your own life?

I am not expecting the end of the species, nor do I fear it, since that would only contribute to attracting it. I see us on track for making the Love Age a reality. As I see it, we humans are the Divine's experiment. We were given the freedom of choice as well as advanced mental, emotional, imaginative, language, and dexterity skills. Combine these with having the conscious power of the Divine Self for using intentions and the awareness to know what is good-for-All, and you'll know the power we have to help make changes. Humans truly seem to be an experiment in testing whether we will choose LoveAge-creating to change the ego consciousness. We will consciously have to decide to partner with the Divine to continue our survival, or we will become an extinct species of the 99.9 percent club.

We can no longer rely on dogmatic scientific models in which evolution is based on chance rather than on partnering with the Divine. We can no longer rely on religious myths and dogma teaching that God created the earth and life in seven days. Evolution is a reality. Nor are we any longer victims of God's wrath, but we are responsible for consciously partnering with the Loving Source to make love work in the world. We are in charge of the direction of our evolution, and we'll receive the consequences of our choices.

Do you believe humans will be a successful experiment of the Divine?

Table 14.3
Shifting from the Ego to Love Age Consciousness

QUESTIONS	EGO CONSCIOUSNESS	LOVE AGE CONSCIOUSNESS
What is your relationship with the Divine?	Secular/atheist Parent/Child Fear-based Faith/dogma-based Separation from Divine	Spiritual Partnership Love-based Evidence-based Oneness with All
What is your relationship with other people?	Good-for-me Conflict-based Ego protects itself Disharmony Unhappy Victim Separate from others	Good-for-All Love-based Soul loves itself & others Peace & harmony Joyful Responsible for oneself Oneness with others
How do you communicate with the Divine?	Use secondhand sources Worship & rituals Ego's conditioned habits Mental reasoning	Use direct experiences Divine presence Divine conscious awareness Divine Stillness
What are some of the other transitions?	Live in past & future Unconscious reactions Passive victim Imprisoned with *karma* Change others & circumstance Ego habitually reacts Attachment to things	Live in the NOW Conscious intentions Proactive co-creator Free from past *karma* Change oneself first Use conscious intentions & actions Detachment from things
Who am I?	Ego self	Divine self

The next chapter will examine the significance of your committing to becoming a loving being. Your conscious participation is of utmost importance for us to transition to the Love Age. You are highly important in making an historic evolutionary jump into the Love Age, which is how important and significant you are in today's world.

Are you on board?

Figure 14.4

SUGGESTED QUESTIONS FOR PERSONAL AND GROUP DISCUSSION

1. Do you believe we are in an evolutionary period of jump-starting the spiritual era?
2. Is your awareness of pure consciousness growing?
3. Do you use living in the NOW, saying affirmations, verbalizing, visualizing, asking questions, or listening to divine stillness to become more spiritually aware?
4. Do you believe the evolution of awareness is transitioning into the Love Age?
5. Do you believe humanity will actually live the consciousness needed for the Age of Love to materialize?

☺ *Smile* ☺
You are in a major evolutionary jump-start period of change.
Are you jumping with LoveAge-creating into the Love Age?

Chapter Fifteen

Importance of Being a LoveAge-creator

Do you know how important you are? You are a divine being with the co-creative and oneness powers of intentions and love that allow you to direct your life consciously for the good-of-All. By living in a partnership or in oneness with the Divine, you have powers to bring peace and harmony to Earth. You have the power to help co-create the Love Age by just being a loving being in all your personal relationships. Your good-for-All choices could very well be the difference between the ego consciousness continuing to increase conflict, unhappiness, and chances for extinction or having the world thrive as a community of peace and love.

No world leader, athletic star, billionaire, Hollywood star, or spiritual leader is more important than you. As Soul with its power for good, you are equal to all others, and if you use that power, you can be a pioneer for creating the Love Age. That's how important you are.

Do you believe you have the power to help co-create the Love Age?

Your Power of Change

There are powers for change more important than sunbursts, magnetic shifts, Mayan predictions, self-help books, nonviolent actions, or other empowerment forces that can affect the reality of the Love Age. This power is as simple as **YOU** deciding to be a LoveAge-creator for yourself and for family, coworkers, friends, other personal relationships, and the communities that your heart touches. This personal power to change your life is the greatest *co-creative and oneness-creative power for peaceful change* in today's world.

> *Create Love in Your Personal Relationships And Fill the World with Love*

Your power to affect the transformation of the Love Age lies in your freedom of choice. If you consciously choose to be more loving, you add higher energy vibrations to the collective consciousness, and this helps make the Love Age a reality. As this collective consciousness matures, with more Souls joining in, the social evolutionary end point of the ego consciousness will make a significant jump of spirituality into the age of love.

> *Changing Yourself Changes the World Too*

I once thought social change was limited to changing others or to change social institutions by political methods, by converting others to my religious dogma, by violent revolutions, or by nonviolent actions. I have learned that by changing my own consciousness, I serve as a channel for love, which ultimately helps to raise the collective consciousness of the groups with which my energy fields interconnect.

Importance of Being a Love Age Creator

> **FROM THE HEARTS OF YOU AND ME**
>
> *Please...*
>
> *May the cool summer breeze of peace flow,*
> *From deep within the hearts of you and me.*
>
> *May a jolly baby's laugh echo,*
> *From deep within the hearts of you and me.*
>
> *May divine love and peace freely flow,*
> *For All in the Love Age to see.*

Albert Einstein said that "the release of atom power has changed everything except our way of thinking, and thus we are being driven unarmed towards a catastrophe." Will Rogers said that "you can't say civilization don't advance, for in every war they kill you a new way." Technological advancements are useful, but unfortunately, most of those in charge of these technologies are of the ego consciousness, and they use these advancements for wars and greedy purposes. The use of technology needs to be guided by those who live for the good-of-All when solving social problems and co-creating peace and love.

> *Please Change the World and Begin with Me*

Good-for-All Protesting

Albert Einstein said, "You can never solve a problem on the level on which it was created." Trying to solve an ego problem with an ego solution will never change anything. You'll just substitute one ego problem for another ego problem. Solving an ego problem with an ego response is like trying to drive a nail into concrete with your fist. All you'll get is a bloody fist. This happens too often in today's world. We need to solve ego problems with solutions of love or with good-for-All solutions.

The protesters throughout the world desire freedom, peace, opportunity, prosperity, equality of opportunity, happiness, and security, and they are beginning to make authoritarian leaders and good-for-rich economic corporations and institutions aware of their desires. People want the freedom to choose their own destinies. They want these things rather than being subjected to greedy, authoritarian leaders and to the rich, who exist to serve themselves whether it is in a capitalist or communist, developed or undeveloped society.

The gap and conflict between those who have and those who do not is continuing to increase in the current jump-start period. Increased inequality creates conflicts and protests, which can lead to positive changes or to increased violence and simply replacing an old suppressive regime with another one similar to it. Conflict is not an evil in itself; the evil depends on how a conflict is responded to by the members of a society and its leaders. The key is whether a society handles conflicts with the ego or with a Love Age consciousness in order to make a better life for all.

Unfortunately, today's protesters too often become tomorrow's dictators. The ego consciousness and its revolutions create violence and destruction, and the victor controls a new society for the good-of-me (victor). This change simply results in one ego-controlled government replacing another with different ego leaders and groups receiving the benefits. This is the concern the world has about the Arab Spring, during which it appears that different ego despots will force their beliefs, authoritarian governments, or religion on others rather than giving freedom and operating for the good-of-All.

Importance of Being a Love Age Creator

The question is this: *What direction will the social evolution of the human ego take?* Will it exist for the good of the few rich and powerful egos or for the good-of-All? Right now, it is for the few, and if this continues, it will be for the good of nobody.

If protests are needed, they will hopefully use the power of love and peaceful practices, which are guided by their divine partners to implement good-for-All solutions. If this is done, then peace, equality, freedom, and happiness will bring about the age of love, rather than merely elevating a different ego protesting group's desires for wealthy, for religious control or for political power.

Are the protests for change throughout the world a sign of the collapse of the Ego Age?

We will never have good-for-All protesting unless the people who are protesting are increasingly being more loving in their own lives. This requires filling hearts with love and peace first, from which solutions of love and peace can flow. If you're not filled with peace and love, it will be difficult to know how to protest peacefully or to create solutions of love.

Good-for-All Protesting Requires a Peaceful & Loving Heart

Are you filling your heart with love and peace to help bring about the age of love?

I'm not suggesting that the Love Age does or does not need protests or that you should get involved in them. This is a decision that each individual needs to make about how they will use their lives to advance love in the world. Most will probably just focus on practicing love in their own personal lives, which is the starting place for the Love Age while others will feel led to practice love in other kinds of activities.

Some may be led to serve the poor, animals, or environment. Others may get involved in political elections and leadership, improving family life and education, improving the health system, changing the economic system for the good-of-All, spread the Love Age message, and thousands of other ways of getting involved in the changes to come. These decisions of loving service to get involved will arise from deep within your heart and require a deep level of commitment and love.

The Love Age Commitment

The change needed for the age of love is for you to commit to moving beyond your current level of creative empowerment by taking small steps toward LoveAge-creating. If you are not ego-realized, it is important to start working on achieving this phase by recognizing your ego habits, replacing them with Love Age habits, living in the divine presence so you can be guided by its wisdom, and being the Divine's co-creative partner. By initiating a Love Age commitment and transforming yourself, you'll help move the world forward. Otherwise, your lack of commitment will make for one less energized Soul, which will make it more difficult for the Love Age to advance. Being a co-creator of love starts now, and the process will continue during every present moment of your life.

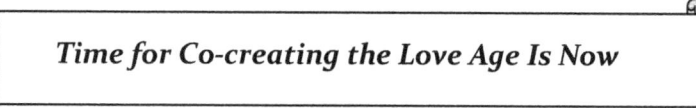

Time for Co-creating the Love Age Is Now

Are you now committed to replacing ego's habits with new habits of love?

It doesn't matter how many times you have tried or committed to being a more loving or spiritual being in the past,

Love Age Commitment

I _____
     (Say Your Name)
commit to...

- ☺ Recognize my ego habits and fears, take responsibility for them, and replace them.
- ☺ Be aware of myself as the Divine Self and the spiritual energy being that's one with All.
- ☺ Co-create peace, joy, and love in all my personal relationships.
- ☺ Be the love I already am by loving myself as well as the All.
- ☺ Be aware of divine wisdom's guidance.
- ☺ Use the power of Soul, mind, feelings, and imagination to co-create good-for-All intentions.
- ☺ Recognize, replace, and allow what's good-for-All.
- ☺ Feel worthy of the Divine's material and spiritual abundance.
- ☺ Be one with the Divine and with all life.
- ☺ Live the love Jesus, Buddha, and other enlightened Souls practiced.
- ☺ Partner with the Divine and with others to co-create the Age of Love.
- ☺ Take 30 seconds a day and ask divine wisdom, what small thing can I do today to be more loving?

Your Creative Power of Love

without having the success you desired. Just use the common sense approach—*"If I mess up six times, try it seven times and so on."* Since spiritual energy has increased in recent decades, you are living in a time when it will be easier for you to be a more powerful and loving being.

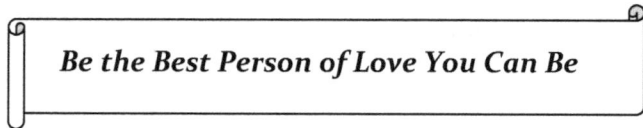
Be the Best Person of Love You Can Be

The shift in consciousness needed for the Love Age depends on you. You cannot wait around and let the destructive ego consciousness continue to gain in power and be increasingly more difficult to change later. The time for change is now. It will not be done for you. It requires commitment and help from people like you who are interested enough to read this book and to be more loving.

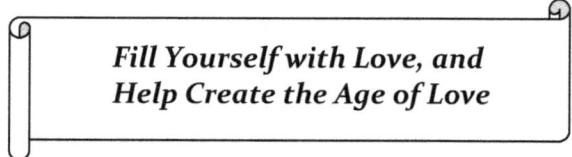
Fill Yourself with Love, and Help Create the Age of Love

You can use the "Love Age Commitment" as a guide or affirmation, to help keep your attention on the desire for energizing your Love Age life. Select one or several of the commitments and repeat it aloud in the privacy of your home or out in the peacefulness of nature. You can also tape the Love Age Commitment on the wall where it will remind you of your commitments. You can cut out the copy of this commitment found in Appendix A, or you can find the "Love Age Commitment" on the Internet at www.tommyknestrick.com where you can print a copy for yourself.

If you want to use the commitment, sign your name in the blank space, record the date, add additional commitments if you desire, cross out the ones you do not want, and hang the page on a wall to help keep your commitments fresh in mind. You can also make a completely new commitment for yourself. It will help direct your attention toward being a co-creator with love and will energize your intention to materialize the changes you want for your own life.

Make the "Love Age Commitment" yours. The one I'm proposing is mine. I hope you realize by now that the consciousness shifts that I went through and the changes I made in my life arise out of my life experiences. I'm simply proposing them for you to evaluate whether they are something you may want to use to create your life with love.

Are you committed to being a more loving being???

This commitment is not meant to be a set of rules for the Love Age or to be a substitute for you creating your own commitment. Love Age creators are masters of their own lives and destinies so commit to whatever is best for you. Use the commitment if it is useful, or change it to suit what you want for a commitment.

Social Relationships Are a Proving Ground for Love

The social environment and relationships with others are the main proving grounds for the practice of love. In Eckhart Tolle's book, *The Power of Now*, he has a section entitled, "Relationships as Spiritual Practice." He uses the relationship between men and women as an example of how the ego "mode of consciousness and all the social, political, and economic structures that it created" have entered "the final stage of collapse."

When I wrote this current chapter, I was attending the Sacramento book discussion group that met at a local Catholic Church, and we discussed Tolle's section on "Relationships as Spiritual Practice." The discussion of how relationships were helping the members made me realize the importance of relationships for spiritual development.

One morning while still in the state of twilight sleep, a state between sleeping and being aware, thoughts poured through my mind from an inner source about how social relationships were proving grounds for spirituality. Relationships serve as a school for testing and learning how to be more loving.

Learning spirituality is done best in families, at work, or in other social relationships rather than through secluding yourself in a monastery, ashram, or cave. Life in regular society is where the conditioned mind of the ego is in charge and where you can learn to overcome its dominance. Social relationships are your testing grounds for recognizing ego habits and for using the co-creative or oneness-creative ways to replace them.

Is the ego mind or your spiritual self in charge of your relationships?

***

I saw an outdoor church sign that said, "We Can Help You Study for Your Final Exam." I thought to myself, there really are no final exams to go to heaven or be spiritual; there are only daily pop quizzes. Recognizing ego habits and replacing them with loving habits happens randomly in daily relationships with others, which are your tests for learning to co-create with love.

***

You are now living in the information age, and it, too, has brought problems. We have accumulated extensive knowledge, and we can share it quickly, even worldwide, over the Internet. Unfortunately, this abundance of information can also become overwhelming and distracting. Knowledge is power, and it can be used either for the greater good or for controlling others for personal gain. Fortunately for us, the Internet can also serve as a web of love for the Love Age.

That is why the egos of dictators or greedy rich people of the world want to control what their people can access on public media or on the Internet. It is also why political leaders and the rich in America like to control the content of the news and even buy TV and radio stations, magazines, and newspapers to broadcast their own propaganda. The freedom of the press, one of the cornerstones of democracy, is being seriously threatened.

I had a subscription to *Newsweek* magazine. One day, I opened it up to read what I thought was going to be an objective account of the news, and all I found was a right-wing interpretation of it. I cancelled the subscription and wondered how far those holding the politically extreme views will go to control the media.

Those who do not want change are usually the ones using propaganda and fear to control the information people receive. They are not concerned about evidence, since they only communicate what serves their ego's dictates and its greedy desires. This is why America's forefathers were so concerned about the freedom of the press, and it is why we should be too. To function properly, democracy needs objective news and evidence-based information to help its citizens do what's good-for-All.

The mind and its ego consciousness are poor sources for spiritual guidance, but they are highly useful under the guidance of divine wisdom. When science, reasoning, technology, economy, government, and social relationships are guided by divine love and wisdom, they will move us into higher, more harmonious and good-for-All relationships, institutions, and living.

Do you use divine wisdom to guide your life for the good-of-All?

Operating with soul awareness in control of your life brings the power of love into social relationships. You will leave behind the conflicting behavior of the reactive mind and will replace this behavior with what's good-for-All. Putting love into relationships makes the Love Age flourish and thrive. There is no need for worship services since your feet are already in a sacred place where you can live your daily relationships with love and can pass life's pop quizzes.

> **Relationships Are Opportunities for Giving and Receiving Love**

Simple acts of smiling, hugging, touching, random kindness, recognizing and controlling ego reactions, and bringing humor into your relationships put love into your life. Relating to others with divine wisdom and love is proof that you have evolved into the spiritual dimensions of love. This is a choice you have to make if you want love in yourself and in the collective consciousness of your groups.

Are your relationships thriving on divine wisdom and love?

You Are Your Own Master

Being spiritual means being a master of your own destiny by partnering with or being one with the Divine. No priest, guru, group, church, spiritual entity, or spiritual leaders need stand between you and your life of love or spirituality. You have a direct connection with the Divine and with its wisdom. This is what you must ultimately rely on. Others may help you understand, and the Divine often directs you to read books, but you need not rely on a religious organization, an author, this book, or any spiritual leader for your enlightenment.

> *"God Has No Religion"—Mahatma Gandhi*

The potential organization and structure of the Love Age will most likely be much different from that of current religions. This change is already taking place in America where the fastest growing segment of the population consists of people who belong to no religious group and just consider themselves spiritual. They mix and match spiritual beliefs from the East and the West with their own spiritual experiences in order to create their own personal form of spirituality. This trend is a social movement of spirit and love in America. It is also occurring throughout the rest of the world.

In 2008, the researchers at the Pew Forum on Religion and Public Life placed this segment of people at 16.1 percent in the United States. In the 18–29 age group, the number was at 25 percent. This indicates that as these younger people grow older, this trend will continue to increase. I also believe that as the baby boomer generation retires, more of its members will take up their old commitments and become more loving and spiritual. I recently read in an AARP publication that the baby boomers are turning to spiritual concerns once they retire. They may give a significant boost to those committed to the Love Age.

> ***Follow the Divine Within,***
> ***Rather than Following the Leader***

I recently visited my family in Pennsylvania and heard that the local Methodist Church I attended and another one nearby were scheduled to be closed. Churches are not attracting the youth, and they are slowly dying. If a young person is still attending church, he or she is more likely adhering to a different religion than their parents. The Catholic religion is decreasing in membership in the United States, but this decrease was offset by immigration from Mexico and other countries until the "great recession" caused high unemployment, which caused them to exit the country. These are the changes that are facing organized religions. They will have to change their dogmatic approach to religion and establish a more direct and loving relationship with the Divine if they are to serve the need for love in the new age.

Rob, my oldest son, always disliked organized religions. If any of you are like him, you'll find that the new spirituality is about as disorganized and individualistic as it comes. Most of the spiritually enlightened will be without any churches or a central organization. There will most likely be loosely organized workshops, retreats, protests, and seminars or conferences. The "Occupy movement" for example has an individualized structure that will most likely be the predominate way of operating in the Love Age.

Educational centers, retreats, and healing centers will probably exist, but there will be no central location or administrative building to organize and guide the Love Age. Small discussion groups that meet in homes to discuss spiritual books or talk about issues along with a diverse selection of spiritual leaders will be the predominant backbone of the Love Age. This was how Christianity originally existed and thrived until organized religious leaders took over control and banned the *Gnostic* groups and their gospels, who practiced a more direct and mystical relationship with the Divine.

The Love Age organization will not have a central leadership such as popes, bishops, priests, monks, clergy, rabbis, or ministers. There will be multiple spiritual leaders providing guidance and spiritual people like you following your inner guidance to select what is best for your own spiritual enlightenment. You and others will guide your lives with good-for-All intentions, love, and actions.

The diversity of beliefs within and without the Love Age groups will require a high degree of tolerance, respect, and love for each other. You will need to pick and choose from available spiritual paths in order to create your own spirituality. Your path will most likely be one that is lived in partnership with the Divine in everyday relationships and guided by direct experiences and love. The reliance on secondhand sources of dogma, rituals, faith, sacred books, symbols, organizations, or a need to evangelize will no longer be needed.

Just don't be attached to your spiritual path or belief, as though it is the ultimate truth for everyone, or try to force it on others as the ego would do. Any path will do as long as it leads you to be the best spiritual being of love you can be. Make it a path of living with love, and others will be interested in what you have found and will want it for themselves. Spirituality of love grows by your being an example of it.

> **Spirituality Takes Place Wherever Your Feet Are Located**

There will probably be no worship services, membership fees, or tithing. Spirituality and divine presence will arise out of the daily relationships with families, work, friends, communities, and other social relationships. Your example of love in relationships will serve as an advertisement for how to be spiritual.

The poem, "Sermons We See," provides the kind of example of how spreading one's spirituality can be done in the Love Age. Just be a sermon in action. The poem below is only a small section of Edgar Guest's poem, which I've liked since I read it in college.

> ### Sermons We See
>
> **Edgar Guest**
>
> *I'd rather see a sermon than hear one any day;*
> *I'd rather one should walk with me than merely tell the way.*
>
> *The eye's a better pupil and more willing than the ear,*
> *Fine counsel is confusing, but example's always clear;*
>
> *And the best of all the preachers are the men who live their creeds,*
> *For to see good put in action is what everybody needs....*

[Source: www.sofinesjoyfulmoment.com/quotes/sermon.htm]

The Love Age will not rise out of the ashes of the social/technological era of its own volition. It requires your conscious commitment. If you can't feel or see yourself as a being of love, the Love Age may never happen. The Love Age will be attracted by the power of loving intentions. Being a co-creator of love in all your relationships with the Divine and with others is the foundation for building a new world and realizing the age of love.

If You Want a Changed World, Give It a Loving You

The only reason you're not now a loving spiritual being is that you do not wholly intend, expect, or commit to being it. You are responsible for your choices and I am for mine, and these choices will determine whether the next major era in the evolution of awareness happens. Spirituality is important for your own life's happiness as well as for the Love Age. If you want a changed world, give the gift of a spiritual you of love to it. This is how important you are. If you want your life to have purpose, you have to look no further than being a loving human being.

Are you willing to allow the Divine help you make a difference on this planet?

Whatever effort you can do to make the changes happen will combine with the Divine Energy of others to create a force stronger than you can imagine for peace, love, freedom, and joy. Please, be and do as much as you can to activate your creative power of love.

How Can You Be a LoveAge-creator?

Throughout this book I have dealt with the changes in consciousness you need to make in order to be a LoveAge-creator, but I have said less about *how* to do it. This is a topic that requires another book, but at this time, I want to summarize

Importance of Being a Love Age Creator

some of the things to start you on being a LoveAge-creator of your own life.

Recognize It

There is a spiritual principle that if you ask the Divine a question, you will receive an answer. Try it and see if it works when you have a few free seconds during the day or during meditation. You can ask a question about recognizing your ego habits and fears.

1. For example, *ask*, What ego habit do I need to change first?

2. *Watch and listen* throughout the day for the Divine to provide an answer. It may be from a song (e.g., "All You Need Is Love"), dream (e.g., Amanda dream), gentle insight (e.g., "go to the local book store"), tree, book, meditation, knowingness, etc.

3. When you recognize a habit that needs changed, *ask and listen for an answer to...* What is the fear that underlies this ego reaction?

4. Accept *responsibility* or ownership of the ego habit and fears and *be committed* to changing them for the good-of-All.

Replace It

Habits and fears operate in an unconscious mode, and once they are recognized, it is time to consciously choose a replacement habit, state of being, or action. Change occurs by replacing an unconscious reaction with a conscious action of love. Since energy flows where focused attention goes, you need to consciously focus on love. How do you focus attention on what you want to be?

1. Establish an *intention, commitment, or set goals* for what you want to be.

2. Use **thoughts, feelings, and visualizations** to focus energy on intentions.

3. Use **affirmations** like, "I'm love," to focus attention on an intention.

4. Just **BE** what you already are as Soul. Think, feel, and imagine being a creator of love.

Allow It

Allow the Divine to be your partner, to guide you, and to co-create what is good-for-All. There is a social principle that the best way to change your habits or your life is to take small steps. Just take 30 seconds, first thing in the morning or when you have down time (for example, when waiting in line for service), and ask the Divine.

1. *What small thing can I do today to be more loving?*

2. **Thank** the Divine for already answering you request.

3. Be **vigilant** for the Divine's directions.

4. At the end of the day, **record your loving action(s)** in a journal. Do not feel that you should only do one act of love today since the more you do, the higher your vibrations of love will be. If you review these actions at the end of the month, you will have concrete proof that you are indeed being more loving. This in turn will help you be more motivated to continue to raise your vibrations of love.

For most, it's the small steps that will lead to spirituality and the mastery of your ego and life. So goes your teeny-tiny steps of being more loving; so goes the planet's likelihood of co-creating the Love Age. That's how important you are.

Can you make a 30 second per day commitment to make a better life of love for yourself and the world???

Figure 15.2

SUGGESTED QUESTIONS FOR PERSONAL AND GROUP DISCUSSION

1. Do you feel you are a pioneer of the Love Age?
2. Do you believe you can affect the collective consciousness by changing your own consciousness?
3. Are you willing to make small progressive changes in your personal relationships to help bring about the Age of Love?
4. Are you going to commit and exert the energy necessary to help shift us into the Love Age?
5. Have you committed yourself to doing what is necessary to become spiritual by receiving the Divine guides for doing what's good-for-All?
6. Have you committed yourself to the Love Age Commitment?
7. When you intend something, do you expect it or visualize being it?
8. Do you allow the Divine to determine how, when, where, and what your intentions will co-create?
9. Are you committed to replacing ego habits to help bring about the Love Age?
10. Do you use divine wisdom to guide your life for the good-of-All?
11. Are you your own master?
12. Can you handle loosely organized spirituality and tolerate diverse spiritual groups?
13. What is your vision of the Love Age?
14. Are you committed to giving the world the gift of a spiritual you?
15. Are you being the best example of love that you can be?

Your Creative Power of Love

Appendix

Love Age Commitment Form

Love Age Commitment

I _____ commit to...
    (Write your name)
Date: _____

- ☺ Recognize my ego habits and fears, take responsibility for them, and replace them.
- ☺ Be aware of myself as the Divine Self and spiritual energy being that's one with All.
- ☺ Co-create peace, joy, and love in all my personal relationships.
- ☺ Be the love I already am by loving myself and the All.
- ☺ Be aware of divine wisdom's guidance.
- ☺ Use the power of Soul, mind, feelings, and imagination to co-create good-for-All intentions.
- ☺ Recognize, Replace, and allow what's good-for-All.
- ☺ Feel worthy of the Divine's material and spiritual abundance.
- ☺ Be one with the Divine and with all life.
- ☺ Live the love Jesus, Buddha, and other enlightened Souls practiced.
- ☺ Partner with the Divine and with others to co-create the Age of Love.
- ☺ _____
   _____
- ☺ _____
   _____

- ☺ Take 30 seconds a day and ask divine wisdom, what small thing can I do today to be more loving?

Love Age Commitment

I _____ commit to...
  (Write your name)
Date: _____

- ☺ *Recognize my ego habits and fears, take responsibility for them, and replace them.*
- ☺ *Be aware of myself as the Divine Self and spiritual energy being that's one with All.*
- ☺ *Co-create peace, joy, and love in all my personal relationships.*
- ☺ *Be the love I already am by loving myself and the All.*
- ☺ *Be aware of divine wisdom's guidance.*
- ☺ *Use the power of Soul, mind, feelings, and imagination to co-create good-for-All intentions.*
- ☺ *Recognize, replace, and allow what's good-for-All.*
- ☺ *Feel worthy of the Divine's material and spiritual abundance.*
- ☺ *Be one with the Divine and with all life.*
- ☺ *Live the love Jesus, Buddha, and other enlightened Souls practiced.*
- ☺ *Partner with the Divine and with others to co-create the Age of Love.*

- ☺ _____
     _____
- ☺ _____
     _____

- ☺ *Take 30 seconds a day and ask divine wisdom, what small thing can I do today to be more loving?*

Contact Information

For information about future publications, ordering books, book deals, products, workshops, seminars, conferences, and other Love Age activities, please use www.TommyKnestrick.com.

To order products through the mail you can use the following address:

Love Age Press
P. O. Box 292987
Sacramento, California 95829

Index

1

1960s, 15, 156, 202, 204, 211
1962, 202
1998, 87, 202, 204

2

2012, iv, 88, 193 - 211
2016, 201 - 204
2062, 202
26,000-year cycle, 201, 202

A

academic institutions, 57
affirmations, 126, 171, 173, 189
alignment, 201, 202, 204
All You Need Is Love, 1, 127, 129
Amanda, vii, 96 - 108, 121, 122, 126, 129, 159, 169, 171
  worthy to be loved, 93
anger, 50, 101, 102, 106, 107, 113, 139, 144, 166
Arab Spring, 228
Armageddon, 197, 199, 209
atoms, 62, 63, 67, 69, 77
attachment, 39, 41, 42, 44
attention, 1, 20, 30, 33, 36, 61, 68, 75, 103, 118, 119, 173, 174, 176, 181, 182, 189, 203, 210, 232
Audrey, v, viii, 34 - 37, 41, 73, 74, 97, 98, 99, 103, 105, 117, 118, 128, 169, 170, 184, 205
aura, 72 - 76
awareness, 1, 15, 20, 56, 58, 95, 96, 145, 167, 172, 174, 176, 207, 213 - 223, 239

B

Bannerjee, 86
Bhaerman, Steve , 49, 215, 217, 220
Bible, 26 - 28, 57, 58, 152, 153, 197
Biophotonics, 78
blind faith, 1, 28, 153

C

Camping, Harold , 197
Carroll, Lee , 69, 86, 87, 206, 209, 215, 217, 220
Cayce, Edgar , viii, 15, 73, 74, 169, 170, 197
chakras, 22, 84, 85
Christian, 14, 18, 27 - 30, 43, 47, 53, 55, 60, 76, 147, 156, 175, 197, 199
Christian terrorists, 147
co-create, viii, 1, 20, 72, 123 - 127, 173, 182, 184, 192, 204, 209, 215, 220, 225, 231, 245
co-creating, 20, 178, 183 - 189, 192, 220, 227, 234
Co-creating, 125, 130, 133, 182, 183, 184, 186, 192, 230
co-creators, 210
Co-creators, 184
collective, 1, 30, 59, 62, 72, 84, 86, 130, 149, 153, 164, 177, 183, 203, 204, 226, 235
commitment, 243
community, 31, 72, 178, 216, 218, 225
complaining, 32 - 36, 40 - 46, 50, 143, 166, 172, 173, 176
complaining/guilt relationship, 34, 166
conflict, 1, 27, 30, 31, 32, 37, 51, 69, 79, 91, 103, 104, 106, 111, 118,

136, 137, 138, 141, 143, 167, 196, 203, 210, 211, 218, 219, 225, 228
conflicts, 31, 89, 95, 111, 129, 167, 202 - 208, 210, 216, 219, 221, 228
consciousness, 1, 11, 14, 19, 25, 26, 30 - 33, 37, 42 - 48, 54, 59, 61 - 63, 69, 74, 75, 82 - 91, 95, 97, 100 - 107, 111, 116, 122, 123, 126, 127, 130, 136, 138, 142 - 146, 151 - 157, 164, 168 - 170, 174, 176 - 178, 181 - 193, 196 - 221, 225 - 228, 230, 233, 235
cooperation, 1, 70, 89, 104, 111, 219, 220
corporations, 31, 221, 228

D

Dale, Cyndi , 77, 78, 83, 85
death, 20, 27, 32, 41, 42, 50, 54 - 57, 95, 128, 142, 143, 148, 169
destruction, 1, 67, 195 - 202, 209, 210, 211, 228
detachment, 39, 40
Divine, v, vii, viii, 1, 11 - 22, 29, 30, 37, 42, 46 - 76, 81 - 85, 96, 107 - 116, 118 - 130, 137, 139, 144 - 149, 151, 157, 159, 164, 168 - 178, 182 - 192, 198, 204 - 209, 214 , 215, 222, 223, 225, 230, 231, 235 - 242
Divine Energy, 16, 19, 20, 21, 22, 63, 68, 82, 112, 116, 122, 127, 171, 174, 175, 191, 206, 214, 240
divine love, 1, 11, 16, 18 - 21, 46, 83, 91, 108, 116, 121 - 129, 169, 173, 174, 176, 189, 227, 235
Divine Self, vii, 1, 11 - 22, 30, 42, 51, 57, 58, 60 - 62, 67 - 74, 82, 83, 164, 172, 175, 176, 178, 183, 184, 185, 187, 188, 214, 222, 231
Divine Source, 16, 18, 19, 20, 21, 58, 127, 174, 175, 191, 214
Divine Stillness, 175, 189, 204
divine wisdom, 1, 19, 20, 88, 96, 100, 111, 125, 171, 172, 175, 219, 221, 231, 235

DNA, 71, 77
DNA cells, 71
dogma, 27, 28, 30, 47, 51, 128, 144, 147, 148, 153, 155, 169, 197, 222, 223, 226, 238
dogmatic, viii, 31, 56, 60, 219, 222, 237
Dr. Oz, 70, 71
dream, 96 - 101, 107, 108, 121, 122, 126, 129

E

Earth Dance, 70, 215
Eckankar, viii, 15, 43, 57, 170, 171
Eckhart, Meister , 39
Einstein, Albert, 67, 227, 228
ego, viii, 1, 11 - 68, 70, 74, 79, 82, 83, 88, 89, 91, 94, 95, 97, 99, 100, 101 - 145, 151 - 178, 181 - 196, 200 - 205, 209, 210, 214 - 221, 225 - 235, 238
Ego Age, 1, 32, 51, 192, 193, 229
Ego Era, 210, 213, 220
ego self, 1, 11 - 25, 31, 37, 46, 49, 50, 51, 54, 55, 62, 63, 65, 82, 83, 97, 104, 106, 111, 118, 176, 184
ego-creating, 1, 130, 133 - 138, 153, 160, 163, 164, 166, 168, 182, 184, 186, 191
ego-realization, 51, 133, 163, 167, 176, 187
end of time, 54, 55, 193, 195, 196, 197
energy, 1, 16, 19, 20 - 22, 46, 57 - 73, 76 - 90, 101, 160, 173 - 178, 187, 192, 198, 201 - 210, 214, 215, 226, 230, 231
Energy Beings, 68
energy fields, 16, 19, 65 - 86, 89, 178, 187, 226
energy healing, 76
evolution, 1, 136, 210, 215, 216, 218, 222, 229, 239
evolution of awareness, 216
evolutionary, 1, 32, 51, 69, 70, 164, 193, 211, 213, 216, 219, 224, 226

evolutionary jump, 213
extinct, 219, 222

F

faith-based, 26, 28, 30, 57, 152, 219
fear, 1, 32 - 54, 60, 91, 99, 101, 113, 136, 137, 146, 167, 196, 200, 205, 208, 209, 210, 222, 234
Fear, 39
Fear of abandonment, 41
fear of God, 47
fear of losing, 41
freedom, 1, 14, 21, 26, 28, 73, 104, 127, 133, 160, 173, 183, 189, 190, 196, 198, 203, 210, 220, 222, 226, 228, 229, 234, 240
future, 34, 35, 36, 37, 40, 45, 46, 122, 169, 172, 177, 196, 197, 198, 211, 219, 223

G

Gandhi, Mahatma, 153, 157, 236
Gnostic, 237
Gnostics, 28
God. *See* Divine, Divine Source, or Loving Source
golden light, 59, 61, 74
good-for-all, 1, 11, 104, 105, 107, 108, 112, 118 - 124
good-for-All, 1, 20, 21, 61, 89, 91, 106, 111, 116, 120 - 126, 129, 130, 133, 171 - 175, 182, 184, 186 - 192, 222, 225, 228 - 238
good-for-me, 1, 31, 89, 91, 96, 103 - 107, 111, 124, 125, 139, 144, 145, 152, 191, 218, 221
good-for-others, 91, 95, 96, 103, 104, 107, 122, 129, 146, 152
gossip, 50, 144
greed, 1, 31, 32, 51, 103, 138, 139, 196, 221
Guest, Edgar ,238, 239
guilt, 33 - 36, 42, 50, 54, 103, 104, 144, 166

H

habits, 1, 14, 21, 22, 29, 33, 35, 46, 49, 50, 127, 133, 137, 138, 145, 151, 163, 166, 167, 172, 174, 192, 223, 230, 231, 233, 234, 240
harmony, 1, 14, 20, 21, 65, 70, 79, 81, 89, 108, 123, 124, 145, 175, 176, 187, 190, 208, 209, 220, 223, 225
hell, 27, 31, 32, 42, 43, 169, 170
Huxley, Aldous, 32

I

I am Soul, 57
identity, 11, 14, 15, 19, 20, 22, 25, 26, 29, 30, 36, 40, 41, 49, 51 - 58, 65, 69, 176
information age, 234
Inner Light, 15, 61, 156, 157
intend, 108, 130, 173, 189, 190, 231, 239
intentions, 1, 14, 20, 22, 91, 95, 105, 108, 112, 122, 124, 125, 160, 168, 174, 175, 182, 183, 184, 186, 189, 191, 192, 209, 222, 223, 225, 231, 238, 239
interconnected, 1, 70
intolerance, 1, 30, 32, 144, 196

J

Jenkins, John Major, 201, 202
Jesus, 27, 28, 30, 37, 54, 60, 88, 107, 125, 128, 129, 148, 149, 153, 155, 197, 231, 245, 247
joy, 1, 14, 21, 73, 108, 127, 128, 176, 187, 189, 191, 210, 220, 231, 240
jump-start, 216, 219, 221, 224, 228
jump-start periods, 216
Jung Carl
    Synchronicity, 1
justice, 21, 146, 153, 155, 156, 176

K

karma, 15, 20, 159, 170, 187, 223
King, Martin Luther, 157
Kryon, 69, 86, 88, 201, 202, 206, 207, 209, 215, 217, 220

L

lessons, v, viii, 1, 15, 20, 41, 95, 101, 122, 123, 124, 126, 142, 143, 144, 159, 170, 187, 191, 208
light, viii, 19, 20, 29, 34, 52, 57, 59, 61, 67, 72 - 78, 81, 83, 96, 105, 127, 128, 153, 158, 171
Lipton, Bruce H., 49, 71, 215, 217, 220
losing, 39 - 44, 111, 114, 173
Love Age, iv, v, vii, 1, 11, 73, 86 - 91, 133, 147, 164, 167, 172, 176 - 193, 201 - 213, 220 - 244
Love Age Commitment, 232
love your enemies, 130
Love your neighbor **as** yourself, 107
love,, viii, 1, 14, 16, 19, 21, 22, 42, 48, 62, 68, 78, 83, 102, 107, 117, 121, 127, 128 - 130, 145, 146, 149, 167, 173, 174, 177, 184, 187 - 192, 203, 208, 209, 219, 226, 229 - 239
loveAge-creating, 133
LoveAge-creating, vii, 1, 130, 133, 137, 160 - 167, 172, 181 - 184, 187, 190, 191, 220 - 226, 229
LoveAge-creator, vii, 193, 225
Loving Source, 1, 18, 82, 184, 187, 190, 222

M

magnetic grid, 86, 87, 201
magnetic grids, 86
Marianna, viii, 94, 97, 98
Mayan, 76, 196, 200, 201, 202, 226
me-creating, 133, 136 - 146, 159, 160, 182

meditation, 15, 84, 85, 118, 122, 171, 189
Methodist Church, viii, 53, 141, 153, 197, 237
Methodists, 30
money, 32, 34, 35, 37, 40, 136
Mother Teresa, 148
motivation, 1, 89, 105, 124, 125, 126, 129, 137, 145, 149, 151, 152, 155, 170, 184, 187

N

natural disasters, 1, 208
New Testament, 26, 27, 29, 30, 152
nomadic, 94, 95, 96, 106, 112, 114, 115, 116
nonviolence, 30, 152, 154, 155, 156, 157, 158, 203
Nonviolence, 153, 155, 157
nonviolent, 146, 152, 153, 155, 156, 157, 158, 170, 226

O

oneness, 1, 21, 22, 53, 63, 65, 68, 79, 81, 87, 89, 104, 133, 164, 175, 179, 182, 186, 187, 189, 190, 191, 192, 204, 209, 220, 225, 226, 233
oneness-creating, 133, 164, 179, 182, 187, 189, 190, 192, 220
other-creating, 133, 136, 146, 149, 151, 152, 155, 157, 159, 160, 182
outdoor church sign, 47, 203, 233

P

partner, v, viii, 1, 20, 21, 183, 184, 186, 190, 192, 222, 230
past life, 15, 20, 45, 46, 205
past life regression, 45
peace, 1, 14, 15, 21, 30, 59, 65, 70 - 75, 81, 86, 108, 127, 128, 133, 146, 153 - 158, 167, 170, 173, 176, 187 - 191, 203, 207, 209, 210, 214, 220, 225 - 231, 240

Plato, 61
polarization, 32, 65, 68, 69, 79, 89, 137, 196, 211, 221
polarized, 51, 63, 138
Popp, Fritz-Albert, 77
Power, iii, iv, 42, 43, 46, 53, 58, 85, 87, 144, 177, 206, 215, 226, 233
protesters, 228, 229

Q

Quaker, 15, 30, 55, 156, 157, 171
Quakers, viii, 15, 156, 157, 170
quantum energy fields, 65, 69
quantum physics, 69, 81
Quantum scientists, 1, 19

R

Rapture, 197
Read Amanda Literature, 97, 98, 99, 102, 107
recognize, viii, 33, 36, 40, 48, 63, 121, 167, 178
Reiki, 19, 76, 82, 205, 206
reincarnation, 15, 170, 187
relationships, v, 1, 14, 21, 22, 31, 38, 70, 89, 91, 104, 106, 111, 121, 122, 137, 138, 145, 174, 184, 219, 225, 226, 231 - 239
rich, 31, 40, 221, 228, 229, 234

S

sacrifice, 103, 146, 147, 148, 149, 151
Sahtouris, Elisabet, 70, 72, 215, 220
Scallion, Gordon Michael, 199
Schumann Resonance, 86
secular, 1, 25, 31, 139
Shadyac, Tom, 1
social change, 154, 155, 156, 226
social religion, 146, 152, 153
social sciences, 56, 158
social/technological era, 216, 220, 239

sociology, 30, 94, 113, 117, 144, 152, 154, 155, 158
Soul, 14 - 16, 19 - 22, 54 - 63, 71, 74, 82, 101, 107, 127, 128, 130, 133, 145, 163, 164, 165, 168 - 178, 182 - 191, 205, 214, 215, 223, 225, 230, 231
soul awareness, 167, 176, 204, 214, 235
soul-realization, 133, 163, 168, 169, 178, 182, 187, 192
Soul-realization, 163, 168, 172, 176, 178
sound, 19, 20, 72, 81, 116, 118, 127, 142, 171
Space Shuttle, 119
spiritual, iv, v, viii, 1, 11, 14, 15, 19 - 29, 39, 43, 46, 49, 53 - 68, 73, 76, 78 - 96, 101, 105, 108, 122 -127, 138, 142, 145, 148, 151, 152, 157, 158, 164, 167 - 178, 182, 184 - 191, 198, 201 - 220, 225, 230 - 243
spiritual dimensions, 81, 84, 88
Spiritual Era, 210, 213, 217, 219, 220
spirituality, 1, 43, 60, 74, 87, 89, 145, 148, 164, 190, 191, 202, 203, 226, 233, 236, 237, 238, 240
Spontaneous Evolution, 49, 215, 217
Stillness Speaks, 214, 215
Stranger by the River, 102
subconscious mind, 11, 21, 48, 49, 82, 138
subtle energy fields, 83
survival, 32, 49, 136, 137, 151, 152, 200, 222

T

temple of the living God, 57
terrorist, 22, 23, 147, 148
The Biology of Belief, 49, 71, 215
The Subtle Body, 77, 85
them **or** me, 105
Tiller, Dr. William, 78
things, 1, 19, 37, 39 - 44, 47, 50, 62, 67, 72, 73, 76, 93, 98, 105, 114, 125, 129, 135, 138, 141 - 148, 169,

259

174, 177, 182, 192, 196, 202, 205, 208, 214, 223, 228
time track, 198, 199
Tolle, Eckhart , 46, 53, 85, 87, 164, 206, 209, 214, 215, 217, 233
tornado, 208
transitional phase, 133, 163
Twitchell, Paul , 102

U

Ueland, Brenda, 1
unconditional, 125
unconscious, 1, 21, 22, 25, 32, 35, 48, 49, 50, 68, 101, 138, 145, 151, 159, 167, 168, 214
University of Pittsburgh, 1, 117, 155, 158
unmanifested, 18, 19, 20, 21, 22, 68, 81, 174, 214

V

vanity, 50, 83, 106
violent, 30, 51, 200, 208, 226

W

Wall Street, 31
Warren, Rick , 158
wars, 30, 31, 129, 138, 154, 227
Weiss, Brian L., 45
West Virginia Wesleyan College, 26, 33, 56, 60, 152, 154
Westminster College, 1, 60, 94, 112, 117, 158, 169
win/win, 111, 112, 113, 114, 118, 119, 120
worthy to be loved, 100, 102, 107

www.ingramcontent.com/pod-product-compliance
Lightning Source LLC
Chambersburg PA
CBHW032103090426
42743CB00007B/222